Caroly...

Life is short
but friendship is
forever.

W. T. Jaynes

FEELINGS WITH LOVE AND HUMOR

William T. Joynes

VANTAGE PRESS
New York

To my father who is my guardian angel, and to my mother who conceived in me a love and devotion for my fellow man through love and humor.

Contents

FEELINGS
WITH
LOVE AND
HUMOR

"Feelings with Love and Humor"

"I wish to take you under
    the roof of this book,
that we might ponder and
    take a better look."

"Through tender love and humor,
    I did gracefully write,
transcribing my feelings on paper,
    using every insight."

"That deep desire within me
    to tell all the world,
life can be richly beautiful,
    and not in a swirl."

"Through every day of darkness
    peers a ray of light,
striving to find it daily,
    positive thinking my plight."

"Humor, and a gentle kindness,
    overcoming the blue,
love for your fellow man
    will always see you through."

"So humbly I wish to convey
    my poetic art,
that comes deep within me, and
    straight from the heart."

"Lover's Moon"

"Oh! Gleaming harvest moon,
    shining in splendor and grace,
you beam down upon us with
    such a smiling face."

"It is that time of month that
    lovers sing a mellow tune,
affections for each other and
    enjoying the full new moon. . . ."

"You enlighten the shadows and
    pave the darkness of night,
you churn the restless energies
    that makes a lovers delight."

"I'm caught in a distant gaze
    on this beautiful night,
a man truly in love that makes
    wrong, . . . rightfully right."

"So perfect and beautifully round,
    lovers have to stare,
how anything so large just hangs
    so high in the air."

"You lighten the entire world with
    all your radiant splendor,
so take me full moon of love,
    I'm yours, I surrender."

"My Daughters"

"What a wonderful thing a
        daughter can be,
both are so precious and
        like jewels to me."

"There's nothing quite like a
        daughter's tender love,
when you know it is you
        she is thinking of."

"When you see that special
        gleam in her eye,
that special feeling you felt
        seems to intensify."

"So just what does a man
        get up and do,
when that little girl says,
        'Daddy, I love you?' "

"What do you possibly say,
        do you give a shrug,
when that little angel
        gives you a big hug?"

"So how can a daddy explain
        when he's far apart,
that this daddy loves you so
        and so dear to his heart."

"The Aging Day"

"The creation is the beginning as
        dawn introduces day,
all darkness slowly disappears,
        sun brings forth its ray."

"The sun warms the earth as day
        grows a little older,
awakening the morning flowers,
        life seems much bolder."

"Day is slowly aging and a
        mild summer breeze, . . .
sways the colorful flowers,
        caressing the trees."

"The aging day has grown old
        when dusk is near,
night slowly takes over and
        sparkling stars appear."

"Full moon with all its splendor
        slowly taking its place,
looking at all the world with
        such a happy smiling face."

"Night is gradually ending and this
        day has almost died,
soon day will start over again
        with such dignity and pride."

"What Man Must Do"

"A man must do what he
        thinks is right,
can throw hands up or
        come out and fight."

"The many stumbling blocks,
        sometimes losing ground,
fighting just to stay ahead,
        one must go around."

"To meet certain goals he
        must really strive,
working at his hardest and
        keeping hopes alive."

"The direct approach isn't
        always the easiest way,
but that desire within you,
        increases day by day."

"Others may mock you trying
        to sway your mind,
they have opposite goals and
        far from being kind."

"So stick to your beliefs,
        that lasting trend,
keep right on fighting, and
        fight it to the end."

"Value a Friend"

"When a friendship is too
  frequently used,
pressures the relationship,
  winds up abused."

"A friendship that's one sided
  soon withers away,
one that's not self-centered is
  surely here to stay."

"A friendship that's shared,
  one equal and true,
one doing for the other only
  to be shared by two."

"Look not for the benefits but
  how you might strive,
to strengthen the tie and keep
  the relationship alive."

"One good ole telephone call
  when you're in distress,
can comfort any worry and put
  the mind to rest."

"Male, or female, which ever
  may be your friend,
regard it at the highest and
  guard it to the end."

"Value Life"

"To value life so dearly,
    some will spend it,
others, so deeply depressed,
    will try and end it."

"So many distant obstacles
    one has to face,
it's called everyday living,
    and the human race."

"People seeing no light in
    a darkened world,
puts the mind at unrest,
    a mighty turmoil."

"If only one could possibly see,
    and would appreciate,
the finer things of life would
    lead to that 'Golden Gate.' "

"The world is awfully crude
    and difficult to bear,
but would be much easier if
    there's someone to care."

"The gateway to lasting life is
    loving thy fellow man,
then everyday life becomes, . . .
    'The Promised Land.' "

"Being Yourself"

"Me, I'm no dummy,
    surely not a brain,
mind always open with
    everything to gain."

"For I usually say exactly,
    what's my belief,
straight, and to the point,
    and making it brief."

"Believing in the good things,
    but far from a saint,
for you can never be something
    in which you ain't."

"Just being yourself one
    should always be,
taking life in stride and
    loving it tenderly."

"Being truly sincere,
    surely one would find,
reassurance to the soul,
    and peace of mind."

"So let not your mind be
    toiled in a swirl
for it takes all kinds to
    make up this old world."

"A Growing Love"

"Have you ever wondered how
  your love can grow,
if you never nourish it,
  you'll never know."

"Love isn't just something
  casually desired,
but the true lasting love
  must be totally inspired."

"Two loving always
  with all their heart,
taking the phrase seriously,
  'Till death do us part.' "

"Loving each other tenderly,
  through thick and thin,
not just a physical love,
  but loving within."

"Two hearts totaling one,
  together you survive,
separated you suffer,
  not knowing you're alive."

"So feed your love carefully
  with tender love and care,
and the love you build,
  will forever be rare."

"State of Confusion"

"Can it be you dear
      I really love,
or is it myself I
      am thinking of?"

"Am I so bewildered that
      love isn't there,
a state of confusion,
      in world of despair?"

"Am I so selfish to want
      for my very own,
a person to love where
      love is unknown?"

"Love is affection plus
      craving, and desire,
that one has for another,
      setting the heart afire."

"All want to be loved but
      few ever find,
the everlasting love,
      where love is divine."

"There is lasting mental love,
      physical love as well,
by putting the two together,
      loving is just swell."

"Creation and Sin of Man"

"The beginning of human life
    God made out of dust,
a man he called Adam, and
    put in him great trust."

"A rib from Adam's side
    God created a mate,
was world's first marriage, . . .
    wonderful and delicate."

"They lived in a beautiful garden,
    Eden was the name,
plenty of food to eat leisurely,
    without any shame."

"Forbidden to eat the fruit of
    the 'Knowledge Tree,'
Eve was tactfully lured
    by the Devil's plea."

"Both did eat the delicious fruit of
    the forbidden tree,
and they were punished for
    breaking God's decree."

"They knew not shame till
    God's law disobeyed,
banned from paradise for doing
    what God forbade."

"If Love a Crime"

"If loving you my darling,
    were ruled a crime,
I'd be breaking the law till
    the end of time."

"I'd neatly hide you in
    my lasting dreams,
we'd be forever united,
    after my many schemes."

"If I were to get caught,
    I'd have to admit,
to your cunning lasting love,
    I had to submit."

"I'd always be guilty because
    my love won't die,
I could never reform myself,
    wouldn't even try."

"They can torture me or
    even put me away,
but my everlasting love
    will never ever sway."

"So punish me for this love,
    my everlasting guilt,
for this special love I have
    so sturdily built."

"Decisions"

"Many a tough decision a
    person does make,
can be pretty darn rough and
    make the thinking ache."

"If feelings are hurt due
    to a gut feeling,
it cannot now be altered so
    you send it revealing."

"All angles now openly viewed,
    no chance or doubt,
you have reached a verdict,
    there's no way out."

"Your problem answer not
    always a best choice,
but it's your remedy and
    you've stated your voice."

"The decision you've made
    doesn't please everyone,
it's your sanity to satisfy so
    you get the job done."

"That final selected answer,
    you sincerely did derive,
to balance the tilting scale so
    the brain can survive."

"Why"

"As a little boy nearing
      the age of seven,
my father was called to,
      enter into heaven."

"A boy needing his dad in
      those growing years,
to take away the pain and
      smother those fears."

"Dear precious Lord,
      why did he have to go,
when Mom and I so desperately,
      needed him so?"

"A mom needing love as
      only he could give,
such a wonderful dad,
      why couldn't he live?"

"Mom did such a good job
      in raising me,
she did it with such love,
      grace, and dignity."

"Now I often wonder how
      things would be,
if I had a daddy there,
      just guiding me."

"If you can hear me, Dad,
      I really love you so,
as a man I can't understand,
      why you had to go."

"Where Do You Stand?"

"Do you toil in a gloomy
        world of disbelief,
is it grinding in your mind,
        bringing you grief?"

"Do you ever wonder,
        is God really dead,
or do you really believe,
        he's the 'Eternal Bread'?"

"Look at dear old Mother Nature,
        it's all around you,
believe in God the master creator,
        as so many of us do."

"Does the body hunger daily for
        the bread of life,
or do your many beliefs
        create you strife?"

"Let him come into your daily,
        your wondering heart,
He'll calm your troubled life,
        if you'll do your part."

"God's great creative work
        is never ever done,
till every human heart,
        has truly been won."

"So kneel down on bended knee,
        it's that time of day,
it's never too late to repent if,
        now you kneel and pray."

"A Grandmother's Love"

"Ever journey in time backward,
    into yesteryear,
searching for precious memories
    with one so dear?"

"Going way back into time,
    as a little boy,
a visit with Grandma was
    a wonderful joy."

"What a happy time playing,
    it was for me,
sharing a full summer,
    just Grandma and me."

"Remembering all those times,
    both good and bad,
a lot of special bonding,
    overcoming the sad."

"I can remember watching
    my grandma cooking,
and a hungry little boy just,
    standing there looking."

"Casting aside the past,
    cherishing God's wealth, then
a time of total anguish,
    'cause you've lost your health."

"Moments we shared together,
    were moments of bliss,
now tender moments of history,
    fading like a kiss."

"Never ever, ever, complaining,
        you did your best,
you've earned the highest reward,
        'The Eternal Rest.' "

"Now you've taken your
        very last breath, taken
the final challenge,
        the kiss of death."

"May your mind, body, and soul,
        suffer no more, for
now you've journeyed into
        Life's 'Eternal door.' "

"So now when I gaze into
        the heavens above,
I think of Grandma Joynes,
        her everlasting love."

"Thank you so much Grandma,
        for loving me,
you sparked my youthful life,
        did it so tenderly."

"My Plea"

"Oh! How I adore you darling,
    please hear my plea,
you have touched my heart,
    did it so tenderly."

"You are so far away dear,
    but close to my heart,
my lasting love for you could
    not be torn apart."

"Soon time will pass by,
    I'll be coming home,
to you I will cling forever,
    no more shall I roam."

"Torture me no longer darling,
    say you're mine forever,
I'll love you always and always,
    will leave you never."

"Toast"

"As we sit and slowly sip this
    cool clear wine,
remembering those moments which
    are yours and mine."

"Moments we have cherished,
    are here to stay,
clinging to each other,
    till our dying day."

"We are so content and happy,
    yearning to please,
we do it automatically,
    with so much ease."

"So I make a special toast to you,
    with this cool clear wine,
we shall always be together,
    sharing a love divine."

"L–O–V–E"

" '**L**' is for lasting love,
    my affection for you,
cherishing you always and
    keeping feelings anew."

" '**O**' is for overflowing oneness,
    the unity which we share,
communication between two and
    two that really care."

" '**V**' is for valentine Venus,
    my sweetheart forever,
my devotion to always and
    I pledge to endeavor."

" '**E**' is for enriched emotions,
    a most faithful love,
that's what I'll always have,
    my little turtledove."

" '**LOVE**' is a most wonderful art,
    passion makes it great,
I love you most sincerely for, I've
    chosen the perfect mate."

"What's a House Mouse?"

"Who is it that tries so hard,
    striving to conduct,
an entire household,
    on just a little luck?"

"Who turns shopping into
    such a fable,
being so delicately precise,
    reading every label?"

"Who stretches the paychecks,
    to make ends meet,
always expected to
    stay trim and neat?"

"Who carefully plans daily,
    each and every meal,
while the kids playfully
    destroy their oatmeal?"

"Who washes the dishes,
    sweeps up the dirt,
and gets severely scolded,
    for no clean shirt?"

"Who cooks the evening meal,
    with great fineness,
then turns right around to,
    cleans up the mess?"

"Who always helps when Dad
    can't find his tie,
and who takes over when
    baby begins to cry?"

"Who hasn't the time,
    for a short little doze,
because it's time to wash
    the dirty clothes?"

"Who had to be an updated,
    high school tutor,
and when time arouse,
    a trouble shooter?"

"Who would think of it,
    to be so groovy,
to go downtown to that
    afternoon movie?"

"Who is it that just sees,
    no justified humor,
in a dirty, false, nasty
    dirty little rumor?"

"And just who is it very tired,
    feeling a little frail,
must always be ready,
    awaiting her male?"

"And on the home front who meets
    every daily strife,
yes, you guessed it, it's the
    House-mouse, the Wife?"

"A Hex in the Metroplex"

"It was a sunny day in Texas,
    the sun was rising high,
beads of sweat rolled off my chin,
    trickled down my tie."

"The ticket counter lines long,
    flights showing full,
pair of feet under seat,
    that ain't no bull."

"People standing in long lines,
    'Cool,' but in despair
waiting to buy their tickets and
    to pick a swinging chair."

"Do you want smoking, non-smoking,
    window, or aisle,
we'll be boarding your flight,
    in just a little while."

"No matter what the weather,
    snowing, sleet, or rain,
You've got to get those people,
    on that plane."

"Get all that baggage loaded,
    time has begun to race,
it's hard to be on time if you can't
    keep up the pace."

"It was a hell of a foot race,
    from gate to gate,
the ramp agent desperately trying,
    not to be late."

"The cargo is now loaded,
    so start the show,
the crew in alert position
    and anxious to go."

"One thing about our mechanics,
    they really love it,
when the ramp agent tells them,
    to shove it."

"Dispatching exactly on time,
    is such a delight,
but a total catastrophe if you've
    forgotten to board the flight."

"Bills"

"Ever wonder just where
    that dollar went,
before you've gotten it,
    is already spent?"

"Putting all your bills in
    a large round hat,
drawing just one at a time,
    paying this, delaying that."

"You pinch the feeble penny,
    stretch that dollar,
at the end of the month watch
    the creditors holler."

"That grocery money hidden in,
    the old cookie jar,
just does not seem likely to,
    make it very far."

"With nerves a bit fragile,
    mind a total wreck,
there's just so much to,
    one old paycheck."

"Those expensive school supplies,
    plus winter clothes,
kids need new Sunday shoes,
    mate needs new hose."

"Doctor bills, dental checks,
    the bills bombard,
only one thing to do now is,
    dig out a credit card."

"The old worn out credit card
    sees you through,
what about next month when
    everything is past due?"

"Just can't seem to make it,
    bills have really grown,
you simply consolidate everything,
    then apply for a loan."

"With problems temporarily curbed,
    the mind begins to throb,
what you really need now is,
    a better paying job."

"Going to Town"

"Through very heavy traffic,
    into down town,
looking for a parking place
    and wearing a frown."

"A race to the building so
    you are not late,
you find yourself a seat
    and begin to wait."

"So here I sit patiently waiting,
    in a crowded room,
hoping to be called upon,
    sometime before noon."

"Wall to wall people all
    sitting in a row,
waiting for action and
    raring to go."

"You sit, wait, and listen,
    for your name,
the speaker announces, . . .
    this is not a game."

"The clock on the wall seems,
    running very slow,
up comes a man telling you,
    just where to go."

"Now here's a burly little man,
    who's such a bore,
he up and takes you to the
    very next floor."

"Suddenly a sharp elbow,
    a jabbing nudge,
you suddenly awake to find, its
    only the 'Judge.' "

"You're wide awake now but
    still in a fury,
somehow, you've been selected to
    serve on the jury."

"A Fringe on Revenge"

"Here I humbly sit,
    broken hearted,
trying to figure out
    how it all started."

"The scenery was beautiful,
    the people kind,
you seek some rest and
    peace of mind."

"In the evening it's wine,
    women, and song,
spicy food to eat and
    I'm still going strong."

"All of a sudden like a
    bolt of lightning,
a weird little feeling that,
    surely was frightening."

"Feeling so much worse, the
    stomach starts churning,
becoming frail and weak-kneed,
    with eyes a-burning."

"Noisy bowels were grumbling loud,
    yet a little slow, . . .
as I departed . . . 'Adios'
    Dear ole Mexico."

"Trying desperately to figure out,
    just what I ate,
bowels are now churning,
    a more rapid rate."

"Finally getting myself home,
    was really a chore,
good to be finally at home,
    but yet a little sore."

"It took some time to
    overcome my trip,
was afraid to eat anything,
    just sip and nip."

"Every time I think back on it,
    I really cringe,
cause what I really had was,
    'Montezuma's Revenge.' "

"A Daddy's Love"

"Hey! Pretty little girl,
    I really love you,
sorry dear old daddy,
    has made you blue."

"Many things have happened babe,
    yet so fast,
those unpleasant ones,
    stored into the past."

"But my lasting love for you,
    my little sweetheart,
will linger always with me,
    nevermore to depart."

"As I journey back toward to,
    your childhood days,
you were so precious in your,
    many youthful ways."

"You're now a beautiful young lady,
    growing into womanhood,
learning to do the maturing things,
    a young lady should."

"Soon many things will change,
    you'll have the voice,
of making your own decisions,
    you'll employ the choice."

"Your mother loves you dearly,
    so does your dad,
you can't share both at once,
    which makes it sad."

"When two mature adult people,
　　just cannot get along,
then both must part ways,
　　singing a separate song."

"One very special day soon,
　　as fate will have it be,
we'll share our lives together,
　　with love, you and me."

"You're that part of my life I adore,
　　I cherish so much,
love and time shared together will
　　grasp my dying clutch."

"Searching"

"Could I be so forward
    wanting you in my arms,
just holding you close,
    caressing your charms?"

"Could I be so brazen to,
    completely remissness,
the thought of a tender touch,
    the warmth of a kiss?"

"Could I be so crude to
    want for my very own,
a feeling of closeness,
    to share the unknown?"

"Would I be openly selfish
    holding you near,
using that electricity to
    cast away a fear?"

"Would I be cleverly tacky,
    saying I would care,
to run my fingers through,
    your beautiful hair?"

"Am I so wrong to submerge, in
    the depth of a smile,
desperately to hide away, for
    just a little while?"

"Would you think I'd be so,
    totally out of line,
to seek out lasting love,
    hoping we would find?"

"Could that magic sincerity, in
        those beautiful eyes,
have me in a dizzy trance,
        totally mesmerized?"

"And if you will ever discover,
        I'm just your friend,
will you cherish it dearly,
        to the very end?"

"Life of a Rose"

"Ever watch a forming rose,
    changing by the hour,
turning a tiny rose-bud into
    a beautiful flower?"

"Petals slowly folding outward,
    doing their normal duty,
trying desperately to display,
    its radiant beauty."

"In a youthful full bloom,
    early in the morn,
decorating the glossy greenery,
    covering the prickly thorn."

"Many pretty flowers blooming in
    a marvelous cluster,
is Mother Nature's art and more
    than a mind can muster."

"A rolling landscape of beauty,
    a masterpiece of art,
a heavenly fragrance that
    moves the feeling heart."

"Thousands of delicate buds,
    waiting to come alive,
not knowing the future or
    just how to survive."

"How beautiful they are and each
    tends to flourish,
little do they know that soon
    they will perish."

"Now another vacant spot in
    that growing race,
another forming bud appears,
    taking over its place."

"Death to a fading rose,
    moves in very fast,
when the flower wilts and
    the petals are cast."

"Pain"

"Ever have back problems,
    endured a lot of pain,
your body hurts all over,
    just drives you insane?"

"Have you ever come face to face,
    with that Mr. Death,
that every inhale would be
    your very last breath?"

"Did you ever rely solely,
    on pills every day,
to lessen the pain hoping
    it would go away?"

"Hours of every single day,
    body full of pain,
you feel everything to lose,
    with nothing to gain."

"Months of tests and searching,
    doctors find the trouble,
there's that spark of hope,
    your heart begins to bubble."

"After a lengthy operation,
    then intensive care,
you begin to move around,
    new life you begin to share."

"Teaching yourself to walk,
    do it all over again,
now you feel new life,
    without any pain."

"You still feel weak but
     it won't be long
before the healing completes,
     again you'll be strong."

"Today I am so very thankful,
     I have little wealth,
but I do thank God above for my
     comeback to health."

"You can no longer see the
     pain in my eyes,
the reason I'm here today, is
     My God and exercise."

"The Great Race"

"With skaters now in position,
    you await the start,
crouching on the starting line,
    you're ready to depart."

"On your mark, get set,
    the whistle starts the show.
Last one off the line is
    running a little slow."

"Swiftly around the bend,
    you count the first lap,
you try hard not to foul,
    or have a mishap."

"You cut sharp to the inside,
    trying hard to pass,
you're not in first place,
    but far from the last."

"Down the straight away you
    hear everyone clap,
cheering and yelling you on
    as you tighten the gap."

"With a few laps to go,
    now in second place,
you know if you can last,
    you might win the race."

"It's neck and neck all the way,
    down to the finish line,
pulling ahead into first place
    sent chills to my spine."

"You've reached the finish line,
    you won the race,
you did it with great speed
    and a lot of grace."

"Your hard work paid off,
    now for all to see,
a reward greatly deserved, . . .
    a shiny new trophy."

"Fred"

"There once was a man whose
    name was 'Fred,'
he took a little journey to
    make a little bread."

"He took out a job to get
    out of the red,
and a little extra for his
    face to be fed."

"The job got too tough and
    away he fled,
I'd rather be broke are
    the words he said."

"He had a little fight with
    a man called Ed,
lost his humble life,
    bled in his bed."

"His total action cannot
    be merited,
he cut his life short,
    happiness he forfeited."

"The moral to this story
    cannot be misled,
don't panic, work or play,
    just to get ahead."

"What's Love?"

"True love is the most special
     feeling in the world,
when you're that select man picked
     by that special girl."

"Sincere love is what makes
     the world go—round, . . .
when that special someone you
     have finally found."

"True love is extremely physical,
     true love is mental,
true love is very crude and
     true love is gentle."

"When eyes affectionately meet,
     you feel that craving,
a soft finger-tip touch that
     sends emotions a-raving."

"A tender little caress with
     that sincere feeling,
brings out love and desire
     with affections revealing."

"With lips tenderly interlocked,
     you can taste desire,
that fires up emotions and
     sets two hearts afire."

"Bodies interwoven into a web
     of warm embrace,
full of burning desire with
     hearts a rapid pace."

"When two bodies completely mold
        making love unique,
passion, plus total compassion makes
        true love complete."

"So love your precious mate now
        with all your heart,
each doing their total share,
        nevermore will you part."

"Daydreamer"

"My daydreaming of a beauty,
    normally a bit shady,
but the vision in this dream
    was such a little lady."

"Pure spun gold was her
    radiant long hair,
and as I looked at her,
    couldn't help but stare."

"She had that determined but
    heart-warming smile,
and my heart skipped a beat
    just watching her style."

"She walked towards me with
    great depth in her eyes,
a beautiful charming body,
    perfect in her size."

"I could see the tenderness in
    those ruby red lips,
and a gracefulness in the
    movement of her hips."

"The warmth in her sexy voice
    came from the heart,
truly a lovely creature and
    a superb 'Work of art.' "

"The Motto"

"This new motto is such
   a goal setter,
a brand new slogan, . . .
   'We better be better.' "

"Striving to become the
   airline a little better,
we know the promised goal,
   'We better be better.' "

"On time performance and maybe
   a sunshine letter,
a surge to be the very best,
   'We better be better.' "

"Mechanics so swift and alert,
   like an Irish setter,
flights must be exactly on time,
   'We better be better.' "

"Departments working together,
   an on-time go-getter,
the challenge is now a must,
   'We better be better.' "

"So please do your part and
   don't be a fretter,
the conquest is ahead of us,
   'We better be better.' "

"Don't let this venture become
   a hopeless up-setter,
help with the bosses' promise,
   'We better be better.' "

"Young Love"

"Many a night with you close
    and in my arms,
I held you close to me
    admiring your charms."

"I know it was true love
    at first sight,
but you didn't care for
    what was right."

"Not having your total way,
    you'd always cry,
and here I'd come running,
    just to pacify."

"You knew just how to
    get to a guy,
with that gentle, scheming,
    . . . little sigh."

"You let the world know
    that you existed,
attention came to you fast,
    never being resisted."

"You're quite a little girl
    it's plain to see,
and I just adore you so,
    most tenderly."

"You had always seemed to me
    so brave and bold,
maybe it's just simply because,
    you're three weeks old."

"Death"

"Take not for granted a
    father or mother,
love and cherish them for
    you'll not have another."

"Age is often mean and cruel,
    so I am told,
when that swift aging person
    really gets old."

"Those very rapidly aging minds,
    often making mistakes,
the outcome may differ because
    the decisions one makes."

"All get old very fast but
    they're still in need,
awaiting the mind and soul
    finally to be freed."

"Awaiting so patiently for that
    very last straw,
and from this world of turmoil
    to finally withdraw."

"We never stop to wonder till a
    loved one is gone,
you never miss them till they
    have traveled on."

"Dying definitely terminates
   and death decides
dying is mandatory and
   death divides."

"Death surrounds us daily in
   so many stages.
It takes little consideration in
   the different ages."

"Spring"

"Mother Nature pushes forward
    giving not a reason,
new life begins to form, overtaking
    that dormant season."

"As you feel the warm ultra-violet
    rays of the sun,
your senses tell you that Spring
    has finally begun."

"Buds sprouting so quickly
    upon a naked tree,
covering its leafless limbs,
    with pride and dignity."

"Blades of grass peering through
    a cloud of earth,
giving the fields and lawns that
    feeling of re-birth."

"Birds chirping cheerfully, chattering
    their song of spring,
telling the world of warmth the new
    season would bring."

"Bees exploring vigorously,
    every single flower,
seeking the nourishment of life
    growing by the hour."

"Animals feeling the winter release,
    wrestle in the sun,
for that fight against winter has
    finally been won."

"Life is activated through Mother
    Nature's judgment shove,
always three seasons ahead and
    done with all her love."

"Last Resort"

"Dear sir, just as a last resort,
 I thought I'd come to you,
for I've been sadly knocking heads,
 and I don't know what to do."

"My pride is just an empty work,
 my ego far from bloated,
and I would give most anything if
 I could get promoted."

"I respect the deserved position,
 duty has given you many years,
a lot of blood and sweat, a lot
 of loyalty from volunteers."

"In this past three years sir,
 I've given one hundred percent,
proud of my work and to serve,
 but now my energy is spent."

"I've always surpassed my duty,
 done exactly what I'm told,
this feeling of non-recognition, is
 surely getting a little old."

"So, please view my flawless record,
 I submit my report of devotion,
please consider me carefully, as
 you hand out the next promotion."

"Old Man Winter"

"Please, Old Man Winter, please
    give us a sign,
you've punished us dearly,
    you haven't been kind."

"All kinds of weather this year,
    snowing, sleeting, raining,
everyone was crude, rude and
    always complaining."

"You've stunned the nation and
    frosted the earth,
have dazed all of mankind,
    for all it's worth."

"Take away the cold and hold
    back the blizzard,
we've got to have warmth, . . .
    I'm freezing my gizzard!"

"You make one feel so dormant,
    that inactive feeling,
where are all of those sexy skirts
    with tops revealing?"

"I want to visualize the
    warm soft breeze,
taking over the winter that's
    caressing the trees."

"I want to feel those soothing,
    ultra-violet rays,
that warm all the earth and
    lengthen the days."

"So give us a break, winter,
you've had your fling,
send us a beautiful sign and
please make it Spring."

"Tease"

"You can read my mind with
        so much ease,
we've a lot in common and each,
        yearning to please."

"Those tantalizing dreamy eyes,
        that cute little nose,
that beautiful golden hair and
        fragrance of a rose."

"There's so much to you, I
        can't possibly describe,
but I love all of you and
        want you by my side."

"To contentiously tease me, in
        all my many dreams,
we are finally together after
        our lustful schemes."

"We tease each other in
        our sneaky ways,
when our hungry eyes meet,
        there's that gaze."

"A gaze that lingers on and
        one that is strong.
It feels ah so right and
        yet, ah, so wrong."

"I know I must go soon
        to a distant land,
we shall be parted because
        fate has the upper hand."

"Overdue or Overdo"

"Ever wake up pretty early.
    Body feeling grim,
so you dress accordingly and
    get ready for the gym?"

"First a hot cup of coffee,
    then a little juice,
a brisk jog in the park,
    exercise is on the loose."

"You're feeling pretty good
    just a little plump,
and looking behind you just,
    little too much rump."

"Over the silver belt buckle the
    stomach does drape,
so you do a little extra to whip
    yourself into shape."

"You go through the circuit
    concentrating on gain,
and getting the most out of it,
    go through it again."

"Push-ups, sit-ups, and a
    tennis game or two,
Boy! Do I feel great, feel
    almost like new."

"A hot steam bath, cold dip,
    temperature fifty two,
you come out feeling great,
    but a little blue."

"Relaxing in the evening and
        a might bit tired,
your mind is at ease but
        the body has expired."

"Tomorrow you will awake again,
        little before dawn,
and you'll feel as though the
        body has gone."

"You'll visualize the pain
        within your eyes,
and finally discover, it was
        just too much exercise."

"Distance"

"If I were not so terribly,
    far, far away,
I'd be looking into your eyes,
    this very day."

"As I sit here and meditate,
    drowning in my sorrow,
I'd come to you very soon,
    doing it tomorrow."

"If I could travel into a
    molecule of air,
I'd do it immediately without
    a single care."

"If I could beam myself into
    a ray of light,
I'd do it swiftly and you'd
    be in my sight."

"If I could swim swiftly and
    had the resistance,
I'd come to you no matter
    what the distance."

"If I were a fish in the ocean, I'd
    surely swim to you,
if I had strong wings I'd
    fly as birds do."

"But since I just cannot
    swim nor fly,
I'll catch the next plane
    that's passing by."

"First Sight"

"She was an inspiration
  of sheer delight,
when she first gleamed,
  upon my sight."

"As I saw her upon a
  much closer view,
I sensed the free spirit,
  and all woman too."

"Her tender youth and beauty,
  were her very own,
her fantasies and desires,
  not yet to be known. . . ."

"Her radiant hair was like
  woven spun gold,
and she walked so gracefully,
  proudly and bold."

"She did just everything with
  dignity and duty,
truly a remarkable woman,
  full of feminine beauty."

"Baby! Please touch me just
  one more time,
that my aching heart will perk,
  I'll begin to chime."

"Please hold me tenderly in
  a warm embrace,
watch my heart twitch and
  rapidly to race."

"A Scorpio's Creed"

"To forever endeavor."
"Form your charm."
"Persistence to resistance."
"A favor for a neighbor."
"Lend to a friend."
"A notion of devotion."
"A fashion for passion."
"A duty to beauty."
"Love like a dove."
"Remissness with a kiss."
"Neck like heck."
"Fineness with caress."
"Hate with rate."
"A hinge on revenge."
"Expiring after retiring."
"Die-ing trying."

"My Son"

"My son, who is a mighty,
    strong little man,
will do anything for you,
    and everything he can."

"He helps his mother daily before
    going to school,
does chores in the afternoon,
    honors the Golden Rule."

"Growing every single day,
    getting a little older,
twelve years old and becoming
    just a little bolder."

"When it is homework time,
    he's not a scholar,
but when it's allowance time,
    he looks for that dollar."

"Dirty clothes and filthy shoes
    you'll always discover,
but when it's time for lunch,
    he's such a little lover."

"He races into the house just
    a might bit muddy,
but I love him dearly for
    he's my little buddy."

"So often he is very funny,
    sometimes a bit loud,
but as a boastful father,
    I'm awfully proud."

"Fee . . . Fee"

"My luscious little blonde.
    Pretty as a woman can be.
She's my perfect little baby,
    my Fee Fee . . . my chickadee."

"Eating those special foods,
    watching every calorie,
I love all her charms.
    My Fee Fee . . . my chickadee."

"She knows exactly how
    to keep me company,
she's my flower blossom,
    my Fee Fee . . . my chickadee."

"We master just everything
    in perfect harmony,
my sweet little angel.
    My Fee Fee . . . my chickadee."

"She's my flawless idea of
    a perfect recipe,
Devil-food spice dessert,
    my Fee Fee . . . my chickadee."

"I really do believe she
    is my destiny,
my summation of everything,
    my Fee Fee . . . my chickadee."

"Oh! How I adore her,
    so it's plain to see,
she's my love, my future,
    my Fee Fee . . . my chickadee."

"The Great Surprise"

"For you, Mother dear,
    a great surprise,
you'll never guess it
    unless you're wise."

"These few scribes will
    set you straight,
and you will find out,
    if you can wait."

"A wait that's so intriguing,
    one that's so long,
keeping those hopes high
    and singing a song."

"So if we're blessed soon and
    things go just right,
you'll be a brand new Grandma,
    which is our delight."

"Another Year"

"Today marks our anniversary
 my beautiful wife,
tomorrow is the beginning of
 the rest of our life."

"Another marvelous year,
 has come and passed,
each one just as wonderful,
 better than the last."

"Sharing our lives together daily,
 getting a little older,
kids growing like weeds and
 getting a little bolder."

"So happy anniversary baby,
 I think you're the most,
cause I never do exaggerate, . . .
 although I might boast."

"For you are the one and only,
 I'm dreaming of,
I think of you day in day out, and
 praise our love."

"The Tenth"

"Three thousand six hundred fifty days,
     that's quite a lot,
ten years of blissful marriage,
     today marks the spot."

"Living from day to day,
     watching our kids grow,
a close family relationship, like
     going to a picture show."

"My! How time does fly by,
     so rapid and so fast,
all time being the future,
     no time for the past."

"Not all work and surely
     not all play,
there's a time for relaxing,
     a time to hit the hay."

"A fifty-fifty proposition,
     sometimes more or less,
the other takes up the slack,
     for dedicated happiness."

"We're not always agreeing,
     sometimes even a fight,
then there's the fun of making up,
     for no-one's always right."

"Our art of being close through
     love and communication,
to love both physical and mental,
     without any hesitation."

"Two people working together
        molding a single life,
living to love one another,
        that's man and his wife."

"So happy anniversary baby,
        you've counted to ten,
by working closely together,
        we'll do it over again."

"The Traveler"

"People are now flying who have
    never ever flown,
so many economy fares,
    who needs a loan?"

"Everybody plus their brother
    flying their vacation,
due to the C. A. B.
    Airline de-regulation."

"The Civil Aeronautics Board
    modifying their decisions,
flooding all the airlines with
    many, many revisions."

"The airline industry of today
    has really grown,
now it's hard to get anyone,
    on the telephone."

"Any two people can take
    a Couples fare,
make a selection for smoking,
    or non-smoking chair."

"Keeping those tariffs current
    and up to date,
is just as tough as ticketing, or
    calming an irate."

"With the passenger irritated,
    believing he's abused,
the agent knows the traveler
    is totally confused."

"Because the traveler just
broke the 'excursion,'
management comes in as a
means of diversion."

"All these fare selections,
variety an obsession,
will suddenly change, just
before the depression."

"The Christmas Blitz"

"Do not be so scared,
    have no fear,
for the Christmas blitz,
    is finally here."

"This is the yearly season
    to be jolly,
and Christmas is noted as,
    the grand finale."

"People so restless to depart,
    roaming the halls,
some upset and the rest,
    climbing the walls."

"It is now check-in time,
    so pick a chair,
close the aircraft door and
    put it in the air."

"Instead of a bonus, or
    a Christmas chime,
they just ask you to,
    work some overtime."

"The gate agent's final goal,
    his greatest sensation,
to dispatch the flight to the
    very next station."

"Now the blitz is truly over,
    so give out a cheer,
just get yourself ready for,
    another rugged year."

"So many overtime hours worked,
    you're really tired,
one stiff drink at home and
    you're totally expired."

"Odd"

"There once was a man
    with two left feet,
a shiny little nose and
    a big fat seat."

"He had so many teeth he
    cold hardly eat,
anyone who would see him,
    surely would retreat."

"One eye was blood-shot red,
    the other one black,
he carried all of his marbles
    in a little brown sack."

"He lost his marbles and
    he lost his mind,
I think you'd consider him
    one of a kind."

"He just wasn't very cool,
    nor even serene,
but he was in style
    because it's Halloween."

"Get Up and Go—Got Up and Gone"

"Ever get up groggy,
    just before dawn,
Your get up and go,
    got up and gone?"

"Going to work droopy like,
    a crippled fawn,
get up and go,
    got up and gone."

"Day already half over,
    beginning to yawn,
get up and go, . . .
    got up and gone."

"Work so hard for the
    pay you've drawn,
get up and go, . . .
    got up and gone."

"On your day off just
    forget the lawn,
get up and go, . . .
    got up and gone."

"Taking those vitamins so
    early in the morn,
cause that get up and go has
    got up and gone."

"It's a fact folks and I'm
    telling no yarn,
my get up and go has
    got up and gone."

"Peace of Mind"

"Every human being seeks,
    peace of mind,
most search forever and
    some actually find."

"What a tranquil feeling when
    the mind's at ease,
everything clear as a bell,
    thinking is such a breeze."

"When the mind is satisfied
    controlling all emotion,
the body falls into place like
    an iron-clad devotion."

"The mind controls but always
    in deep mediation,
with the one you love the
    body favors stimulation."

"When you have searched for
    happiness so long,
when you finally find love it's
    gonna be strong."

"To forever be happy, you
    continue to strive,
making every single minute count
    and happiness will survive."

"This is my love, my life,
    I've found at last,
I've challenged the present and
    conquered the past."

"The Big Change"

"You have really changed and
    there's no rebelling,
hips getting much larger and
    tummy is swelling."

"That morning sickness,
    the afternoon nap,
tired early in the evening,
    lemons for a night-cap."

"All these drastic changes, . . .
    no need for alarm,
another human life is
    beginning to form."

"It is so wonderful that you
    can bear a life,
and with God's help, there
    will be no strife."

"With the blessings of God,
    Mother Nature too,
will bring us a healthy child,
    unbelievable but true."

"You have truly changed a lot,
    it's plain to see,
changes that were wanted, and
    always pleasing me."

"So as time passes slowly on
    it's a proven fact,
both working together will get
    your figure back."

"Dreams"

"My dear precious love,
    one I so desire,
you have opened my eyes and
    set my heart afire."

"I love you so much more than
    the beautiful sun,
which lightens the darkness
    until each day is done."

"That wonderful sexy smile,
    those pretty blue eyes,
makes my mind wonder,
    bring forth those sighs."

"My dreams of you are so
    precious and long,
I go throughout the day with
    you in my song."

"Our future looks grim but
    our love won't die,
we are so much in love that
    no one can deny."

"So many crude sacrifices,
    we have to bear,
I think it's fate itself,
    sometimes unfair."

"If fate would just listen to
    my ever pleading call,
you would always be mine,
    my one . . . my all."

"So whatever happens in this
    strange life of mine,
always remember me tenderly,
    and forever be kind."

"What You Are to Me"

"You are a morning star
        shining so bright,
you are a harvest moon
        lighting the night."

"You are the daybreak that
        brightens the day,
you are the sunshine that's
        placed on display."

"You are my protective shelter
        in the rainy cold,
you're that glowing rainbow
        and my pot of gold."

"You are the tender smile
        overcoming a frown,
you are the lasting energy
        when I'm feeling down."

"You are the reflection in
        a soothing daydream,
you are the pretty picture,
        in my painted scene."

"You are my inspiration to
        overcome my strife,
you are the destiny that
        sparks my humble life."

"You are the flowing blood
        surging through my veins,
you are my strength when
        everyone else complains."

"You are my predestination.
     You are my world,
you are my daily sunshine,
     you're my little girl."

"To summarize my feelings,
     you are truly mine,
you are my entire life,
     my love, my valentine."

"A Blanket of White"

"Millions of trickling snowflakes
    on a wintry day,
falling yet so gracefully and
    showing a display."

"Each snowflake falling as if
    drifting hand-in-hand,
creating a beautiful white cover,
    just taking command."

"Like powder-puffs infiltrating
    with flowing grace,
falling tenderly to the earth,
    each taking its place."

"Pearly white beads descending,
    from the cloudless skies,
tiny kisses from Heaven that
    seemed to hypnotize."

"Bushy shrubs and slender trees
    of soft and fluffy white,
towering the open earth with
    a frosty wintry bite."

"Covering the exposed quickly,
    like a giant cape,
being completely in charge,
    taking every shape."

"Camouflaging the frost bitten earth,
    in a blanket of white,
a display of paralyzing beauty,
    glowing throughout the night."

"Night-Night Time"

"Hey there little girl, you're
    beginning to pout,
not always getting your way,
    you begin to shout."

"Sleepy grippe, and tired,
    you cry and fret,
wanting all the attention you
    can possibly get."

"You stump your little toe
    and start to bawl,
mother is there to comfort your
    every little fall."

"Bedtime is strictly taboo,
    you yell and kick,
Daddy gets the paddle and
    you call it a trick."

"Why should I be asleep,
    I did take a nap,
I'd much rather stay up and
    rock in your lap."

"Off to bed you finally go.
    But not really tired,
but soon off to dream-land,
    just totally expired."

"Early to dream land,
    early to rise,
makes baby one step ahead,
    of an early sunrise."

"Sunrise"

"First a dim ray of light,
    slowly peering through,
introducing the morning dawn,
    drying early morning dew."

"A red blaze on the horizon
    striving for height,
steady on a course diminishing
    the shadows of the night."

"A ball of fire peering graciously
    through a darkened cloud,
forcing light into the darkness,
    a tameness becoming loud."

"A spun web of silver clouds,
    like puffs of cotton,
all dimness slowly disappears,
    night has been forgotten."

"Patches of yellow gold woven
    throughout a silvery crust,
a haze of pale blue cream with
    just a touch of rust."

"The calmness of a sleeping city
    changes so at dawn,
darkness disappears as curtains
    of daybreak are drawn."

"A magnificent scene of beauty,
    which seems to energize,
it's dear ole Mother Nature's art,
    a beautiful sunrise."

"Is This the End?"

"Ever wake up believing the
    world to an end,
your head is your enemy and
    you can't find a friend?"

"You fight and you struggle to
    put it all together,
thinking it just can't be you,
    it must be the weather."

"With both feet securely planted
    on a cold bare floor,
you look all around you to
    find the exit door."

"Your body won't respond to
    your mind's command,
your eyes feel like marbles,
    buried in quicksand."

"With a swollen aching head,
    you begin to weep,
for what you think you need,
    is a little more sleep."

"Your system is churning like a
    robot that's on the brink,
now you finally realize that you've
    had too much to drink."

"How Wonderful You Are"

"I owe to you my dear,
    my wonderful wife,
double the happiness,
    you've brought my life."

"You're simply everything,
    anyone could desire,
you manage so easily to
    keep my heart on fire."

"In all my many moods, you're
    still at my side,
a beautiful ribbon in which,
    two hearts are tied."

"You continue working hard,
    keeping a happy home,
always pleasing me like a
    king on a throne."

"You've raised our family,
    did it so well,
never a complaining word,
    we think you're swell."

"You're on duty twenty four
    hours every day,
everything depends on you, with
    very little pay."

"Payment finally comes to you,
    these things you reap,
cause the love you're getting
    hasn't been so cheap."

"Dove of Happiness"

"I placed upon the top our
    Christmas tree of love,
a symbol of our happiness,
    a snow white dove."

"A pure white little dove,
    to show the way,
to give special thanks on
    God's special day."

"Such a beautiful white bird
    guarding our tree,
sitting there proudly on top,
    and so gracefully."

"Its eyes were glowing and gleaming,
    like a new born child,
it seemed to speak to me,
    I'll stay for a little while."

"Oh! Great white snow bird,
    eyes of fiery red,
looking so alive there, how
    about a crumb of bread?"

"Oh! Christmas tree, Oh! Christmas tree,
    please light the way,
so our snowy white bird,
    can guide us each day."

"Our family dove of happiness,
    rules out any fear,
so we'll share our precious dove,
    this and every year."

"This is God's beautiful creature, a
    pure snow white dove,
what Christmas is all about, a
    wondrous gift of love."

"Half of My Life"

"In viewing half of my life,
    a constant working tool,
an instrument of hard labor,
    a complete fool."

"As a driving work slave,
    pleased only by one,
it positively was not me,
    having all the fun."

"A self-induced torture,
    a system of pride,
you're doing it all with,
    no one by your side."

"As a family work horse,
    striving to achieve,
the curbing of family expenses,
    to daily pressures relieve."

"You struggle hard to supply
    a growing family's need,
you're working yourself frantically,
    which seems the family creed."

"As each year fades so swiftly,
    dwindling into the past,
you search your memory, as
    why it went so fast."

"Sinking into a magnetic whirlpool,
　　　of financial quicksand,
a shrewd fight to simply make it
　　　the supply and demand."

"I've sacrificed a hell of a lot,
　　　endured all kinds of strife,
now it's my turn to live, . . .
　　　the second half of my life."

"Memory Lane"

"I want to be with you
    just once again,
to walk hand in hand in
    a gentle rain."

"We'd toast together glasses
    of pink champagne,
as we journeyed together
    down memory lane."

"To cheer you on tenderly
    when you complain,
kissing away the hurt of
    an aching pain."

"Beautiful lasting memories
    will always remain,
to ponder the precious past,
    Omitting the strain."

"Remembering the simple life,
    pure and plain,
sharing the close relationship
    we did attain."

"As you watch raindrops tapping
    a weather drain,
realizing those tender moments
    we will never regain."

"But you hope those memories will
    come once again,
when another journey you'll take,
    down memory lane."

"Lasting Memories"

"She walked so gracefully
    into the crowded room,
pretty like a precious flower,
    pure, and in full bloom."

"Eyes followed her carefully as
    she walked toward me,
all hearts around me stopped,
    and sighed with envy."

"That deep feeling within me
    as our eyes met,
created a most tender sensation
    I'll never forget."

"My heart skipped a beat as
    we sat and we talked,
journeying into the past where
    our memories had walked."

"Memories that were so pure,
    simple, and strong,
like dancing closely together,
    and humming a song."

"As we exchanged our past for
    just a short while,
absorbed in the depth of hazel eyes,
    and beauty of her smile."

"Yes! Those most tender moments
    will last and last,
those beautiful delicate memories,
    dug out of the past."

"Who can predict just what the
    future might bring,
but now is the time to celebrate,
    memories I'll cling."

"Games"

"So many things said, just
        doesn't mean a thing,
a game has been played
        without reasoning."

"Love can be blind and
        create a disguise,
mess you up in the mind,
        unless you are wise."

"When that game you've played,
        brings you strife,
you've lost the true meaning,
        'The Game of Life.' "

"No longer can you say,
        'Birds of a Feather,'
this game you've just played,
        wasn't done together."

"The things you did for love,
        didn't mean any harm,
I was caught in the web of
        a beautiful charm."

"It's so hard to see through
        the game of love,
when it's not yourself,
        you are thinking of."

"It is true, I have lost and
        partially I'm to blame,
but I lost most admirably,
        just wasn't my game."

"Mistletoe"

"Do you ever wonder,
    or wish to know,
about the Christmas tradition
    of 'Ye Ole Mistletoe?' "

"Under the mistletoe, Christmas
    adds another dimension,
and when you see the cluster,
    you know its intention."

"How it gets started growing
    seems such a breeze,
after the autumn has undressed
    its beautiful trees."

"While eating wild berries,
    birds clean their beaks,
on the bark of a tree limb, which
    starts the growing technique."

"A bushy pretty evergreen,
    leathery and broad,
hanging between Heaven and Earth
    placed there by our God."

"There's many legends just how
    mistletoe came to be,
some believe Christ's Cross
    came from such a tree."

"Superstitious thinkers thought it magic,
    and was hung overhead,
to rid the evil spirits and
    protect the homestead."

"The barren women wore necklaces
    to end a dying fertility,
mistletoe bracelets were worn,
    would rid evil ability."

"It shares the qualities of a
    four-leaf clover, a horseshoe,
or the long end of the wishbone,
    or a tender kiss or two."

"Mistletoe may be a myth but
    it's plain for all to see,
it's a symbol of courage, faith,
    hope and, love eternally."

"The Sun"

"On a hot summer day, gaze
    at the pale blue sky,
feel the soft summer breeze,
    watch the clouds drift by."

"The hot raging sun drawing
    water from below,
puffs of pure white clouds all
    aligned in a row."

"It shines down so bright,
    yet almost gold,
it gleams joyfully in the sky,
    so warm and so bold."

"You can feel the heat of the
    ultra-violet rays,
brings warmth upon the earth
    in so many ways."

"The sun cuddles the earth with
    its wonderful force,
goes through each long day,
    steady on its course."

"Many do not realize the sun
    a magnificent art,
God created with his hands and
    touched with his heart."

"So when you look for the warmth
    of the sun above,
think of God the maker and
    praise his love."

"A Walk by the Bay"

"Early in the morning just at
    the break of day,
try taking a little brisk walk,
    down by the bay."

"Down where the shore reaches
    the tall green trees,
you can take a deep breath,
    with a much greater ease."

"So pleasantly fresh and brisk,
    is the morning air,
you'll walk along so lightly,
    without a single care."

"Walking with shoes in hand,
    is surely a treat,
as you let the fine sand sift,
    softly across your feet."

"You see a pretty sea shell,
    one here, one there,
a fiddler crab fleeing for safety,
    you stop and you stare."

"You watch the rolling waves as
    they caress the shore,
each one that comes rolling in,
    caressing a little more."

"Before you realize or know it,
    you've walked half a mile,
not realizing the long distance
    you begin to smile."

"As you look up into the sky
    the sun peers through,
and melts away any signs of
    the early morning dew."

"So you depart the scene, until
    another fine day,
when you can walk once again, . . .
    down by the bay."

"My Little Girl"

"My visions into the past,
  time has really flown,
my precious little baby girl,
  has really, really grown."

"Once upon a time, just
  a bundle of joy,
then a little older,
  'twas a doll or a toy."

"I watched her speedily grow,
  from a tiny little girl,
into a mature precious gem,
  a flawless pretty pearl."

"Many journeys through time,
  those tender years,
a lot of crucial hardships, . . .
  a lot of tears."

"Now a dedicated teenager,
  seeking a skating goal,
heading steadily upward from, . . .
  life's totem pole."

"A lovely young lady with,
  life's journey ahead,
I wish you all the success,
  and the eternal bread."

"Forever my sweet little girl,
  you'll always be,
I'll love you with all my heart,
  throughout eternity."

"Live"

"You can drift along steadily through
    all of your strife,
always wondering where is that,
    relaxing long life?"

"If you always go through life,
    just marking time,
should be reclassified the
    most serious crime."

"How quickly the tendency,
    to forever forget,
the magnificent beauty, of
    an aging sunset."

"How often we earnestly look,
    desperately for wealth,
and in due process completely,
    neglect our health."

"You must live life to the fullest,
    in an everlasting way,
tomorrow will somehow make up for,
    disappointments of today."

"Living life each and every single day,
    one hundred percent.
You'll never totally know when
    your time is spent."

"You need to live your life today,
    for tomorrow you die,
it comes upon you so suddenly,
    giving not a reason why."

"So love your loved ones
    and cherish a friend,
live life to its fullest,
    cherish it to the end."

"The Basics of Life"

"Me, I'm a basic person, and
        what I think is grand,
is walking along the ocean front,
        barefoot in the sand."

"Observing Mother Nature doing
        her normal daily duty,
absorbing the tender life and all
        her marvelous beauty."

"To watch seedlings grow into
        beautiful tall trees,
to feel your face caressed by a
        light summer breeze."

"To witness a sunrise seduced—
        by early morning light,
to share a harvest moon that beams,
        throughout a starlit night."

"To speculate the vision of a
        billion stars in the sky,
planets drifting in the universe,
        would make anyone sigh."

"How marvelous to see birth,
        into this old world,
a tiny little baby crying,
        a little boy or girl."

"Most of the world takes all this
        beauty for granted,
but I, for one, a little bewildered,
        am totally enchanted."

"We should appreciate all life,
  Mother Nature's art,
God created with his hands and
  touched with his heart."

"Super Bowl Thirteen"

"Do those old Miami flights,
    give you the fits,
do you find yourself involved in
    a super-bowl blitz?"

"Many dedicated football fans
    getting out of town,
with victory in their mind, they're
    super bowl bound."

"The traveler excited, cool,
    but not serene,
awaiting kickoff time,
    super bowl thirteen."

"What team will win and who
    will you choose,
one team will conquer and
    one's got to lose."

"Hot dogs, peanuts, popcorn,
    give me a beer,
the stadium is totally packed,
    kickoff time is near."

"Isn't it amazing that at the
    flip of a coin,
tells who gets the football and
    which way you're going."

"Difference of turnovers that
    each team makes,
will be a deciding factor in
    who gets the breaks."

"The number of points at the
  end of the game,
decides who journeys to Football's
  'Ball of Fame.' "

"So relax, this year is history,
  show that souvenir,
then get yourself ready for,
  another football year."

"Near You"

"Just to be near you when
    the lights are low,
to look deep into your eyes
    to find that glow."

"To feel that blanket of warmth
    in your sweet embrace,
to kiss your tender lips, then
    watch the heartbeat race."

"I want to hold you firmly
    within my arms,
and feel the electricity within
    those beautiful charms."

"I want to lay close to you,
    where our bodies touch,
emotions take a journey
    into a lover's clutch."

"I want to hold you close till
    the darkness of night,
is totally overpowered by
    dawn's early light."

"I want to be witness of
    that completed feeling,
which two hearts and bodies
    are totally revealing."

"I just don't want to wake up
    riding a moon beam,
then find out that it's just,
    another wishful dream."

"Growing Years"

"Those younger childhood days,
    the dearest of years,
through grammar school and
    into high school cheers."

"I watched a shy little school girl go
    from basic childhood,
to a hippie teenager and on
    into young adulthood."

"So desperate to finally be out,
    on her very own,
to show all the world she
    has is finally grown."

"Caring for the good times,
    just a little confused,
trying to grow up fast and
    finding herself abused."

"Grasping for love and not
    knowing just how,
experimenting life itself and
    all It would endow."

"A human life is forming now and
    well on its way,
when that toddler arrives will be
    'Mother's Day,' every day."

"A journey into motherhood doing
    what mommies do best,
working both day and night with
    little or no rest."

"When that little baby arrives, I hope
    it cries aloud, . . .
'Mommy, I love you, and I'm
    so very, very proud.' "

"A tear I will shed joyfully
    when finally I see,
that my sweet little girl has
    a grandchild just for me."

"Christmas Eve"

"Christmas eve at the airport,
    all throughout the house,
all creatures were scurrying,
    no room for a mouse."

"Airplanes were filled to capacity
    using the total fleet,
no room for goodies 'cause they're
    all filled with feet."

"Boss controlling the office,
    agents at the gate,
checking in those passengers,
    trying not to be late."

"When out on the busy ramp,
    rose such a clatter.
I raced to the aircraft to see
    what was the matter."

"I looked for the captain with
    a dart and a dash,
I looked for the cause that
    created the clash."

"And what to my wondering,
    eyes should appear,
it's dear ole Santa and has
    pulled the landing gear."

"I heard him sadly exclaim,
    as he left the flight,
'It's been a hell-of-a-day,'
    Nothing's gone right."

"Billions of Snowflakes"

"Billions of tiny snowflakes falling
    throughout the night,
casting a blanket of winter so
    pure and pearly white."

"The moon slowly peering through
    a glitter white sky,
forests and plains of sparkling white,
    seemed to intensify."

"As dawn enriched the entire world,
    sparkling with grace and duty,
kindled by a frosted white shield of
    a spectacular beauty."

"Walking into the brisk morning air,
    breathing with fascination,
through the silence of solitude, came
    this unique demonstration."

"The morning breeze clearing the mind,
    invigorating the heart,
stimulating the entire body giving,
    the brain a fresh start."

"Tree branches displaying a picture of
    puffy white cotton,
telling all the dormant world that,
    all is not forgotten."

"Mother Nature mastered this with
    the greatest precision,
I am so terribly thankful that,
    she passed through my vision."

"Daydreamer"

"I dream of you dear in
     the silence of night,
to hold and enfold you,
     so very, very tight."

"If only you could guess
     how happy I would be,
totally lost in a kiss,
     and so passionately."

"Steadily in my dreams,
     if only you knew,
all my hopes and desires,
     filled totally of you."

"Oh! How steaming my blood,
     beneath your touch,
rushing through my veins,
     bubbling so much."

"If I could just learn to be
     a lover, a friend,
I'd be the one to cherish it
     to the very end."

"Sometime there's going to be
     a Summer, Winter, or Spring,
you will want me close to you,
     and graciously I will cling."

"Now, I am the dreaming poet,
     with nothing else to do,
but writing those tender verses
     my dreams set the music to."

"The New Flight"

"This new flight supercedes
 the 'Three Ten to Yuma.'
It's called the vision express,
 'One Fifteen to Humor.' "

"Scheduled at midday to
 kindle a grumbling morning,
preparing immediate departure,
 tickets issued without warning."

"The flight completely filled
 with smiles and laughter,
nonstop to a happy eternity,
 with life ever after."

"Filling their cups with joy,
 getting rid of those frowns,
filling happy to the brim with,
 comics and funny clowns."

"Letting the fruits of life
 rejoice in daily cheer,
a laugh or a grin helps to
 overpower a fear."

"Finding the 'yell' of happiness,
 a punster being bold,
an overflowing fantasy,
 friendship is oversold."

"Do not delay this flight,
    activate the mechanics of life,
fix it with love and humor,
    dissolve every day strife."

"Humor is not a silly trick, nor
    even the smallest prank,
it's getting the best of life, and
    we have the Lord to thank."

"Totally Confused"

"If you've just decided, both
    mind and body abused,
then it's high time to admit,
    you're totally confused."

"When in this jumbled lifetime,
    you're no longer amused,
then it's high time to admit,
    you're totally confused."

"When you feel that society has
    you completely refused,
then it's high time to admit,
    you're totally confused."

"When you're the accusing and
    also the accused,
then it's high time to admit,
    you're totally confused."

"If when you total your life and
    find your childhood bruised,
strive to overcome it because it's
    your sanity to choose."

"So get rid of that empty feeling
    of being totally used,
look deep within the mirror and say,
    'Me, . . . I'm no longer confused.' "

"Bus Driver"

"Fifty little village idiots,
    crowed on a bus,
nerves a total disaster,
    you're ready to cuss."

"Lots of screaming and yelling,
    pulling of the hair,
full of pep and energy and
    won't stay in a chair."

"You yell, Sit down, shut up,
    they temporarily flop,
but that only lasts till,
    the very next stop."

"So you pull the bus over to
    the side of the road,
you give a little lecture till,
    you practically explode."

"Destination finally achieved,
    relieved but feeling dizzy,
'cause those fifty yelling kids,
    sure as hell kept you busy."

"The last kid finally off,
    you sit back, take a rest,
for tomorrow just another day,
    and another sanity test."

"A Bad Day"

"Ever get up on the wrong
    side of the bed,
feeling so bad that you wish
    that you were dead?"

"That alarm blasting away,
    coming on so strong,
everything in your aching head,
    seemed totally wrong."

"Your get up and go just
    got up and went,
the energy you had, faded,
    from spend to spent."

"Finally, you do get started,
    feeling like a dud,
that morning cup of coffee just
    tasted like mud."

"Any minute now you feel like
    you might doze,
but you try desperately to, . . .
    find all your clothes."

"It's a race to the car with
    little peace of mind,
only to realize the keys,
    you had left behind."

"The vehicle finally running, but
    your battery dead,
if you had only realized and
    had stayed in bed."

"So you rush on to work with
    a hoop and a cough,
only to find out that, . . .
        it's your day off."

"My Swinging Valentine"

"Radiant hair of fiery blaze,
    lips sweet and divine,
the deepest blue starry eyes,
    my swinging Valentine."

"Her complexion was like that
    of a pale white rose,
with sun kisses all around,
    that pretty little nose."

"The beauty of her features,
    perfect was the mold,
casting the finishing touches,
    with a heart of gold."

"A heart so pure and sincere,
    with a lasting love,
she is my one, my all,
    my turtle dove."

"To give her completely up,
    I must decline,
she'll always be to me,
    'My Swinging Valentine.' "

"Typhoon Lola"

"Had been on Guam but five days when
    the radio blasted this warning,
Typhoon Lola is moving on in,
    will hit here tomorrow morning."

"It was the 15th of November,
    '57 was the calendar year,
we assembled ourselves at base supply,
    the typhoon was almost here."

"Men were divided into several groups,
    we had to secure the base,
heavy barrels were propped against doors,
    each man set a rapid pace."

"Dependents were moved into barracks,
    homes might not withstand the beating,
it would be hell to see a palm tree,
    through the roof while you were eating."

"We finished securing all buildings safely,
    and returned to base supply,
I think every man prayed that night,
    hoping Lola would pass us by."

"Bedding was supplied to every airman,
    K-rations issued twice a day,
we could neither eat nor sleep, for
    Lola was well on her way."

"The wind started blowing severely,
    rain coming down hard,
I could hear pieces of tin blowing,
    fiercely about the yard."

"You could hear the wind beating the roof,
	trying desperately to pry it free
power lines were down on the ground,
	everyone was frightened, t'was plain to see."

"Eighty foot tidal waves came roaring in,
	grasping everything within its reach,
villages that couldn't stand the pressure,
	were wrecked along the beach."

"It was over after four days of beating.
	Our work had just begun,
it took weeks to clean up the mess,
	and it sure wasn't much fun."

"Now that everything is back to normal,
	we should kneel and pray,
through all of these past hardships,
	we are alive this day."

"First Flight"

"Put yourself in place of a
      traveler's first flight,
doesn't know just what to do,
      confused and full of fright."

"Standing impatiently in lines,
      nervous, determined to go,
Hey! Give me a boarding pass,
      this line is moving slow."

"As the hostess explains what
      to do, 'just in case,'
a cold chill hits your spine,
      the heart begins to race."

"The old stomach starts churning
      like waves of an ocean,
and looking around . . . you cal feel
      everyone hears the commotion."

"Searching for a good magazine to
      take mind off flying
then coming across a 'barf-bag,'
      you feel like crying."

"After the hostess kindly asks you,
      'How do you feel,'
she then graciously brings you a
      hot steaming meal."

"Flying high above the clouds
      through puffs of cotton,
that Alka-Seltzer you ordered,
      someone has forgotten."

"A brisk rush to the restroom,
    to find it occupied,
desperate for a breath of air,
    and you can't go outside."

"The plane finally landed, you're
    mad, you've had enough,
the captain should have told you
    it would be a little rough."

"Need"

"I need your warming smiles,
    day after day,
I need your love in every
    possible way."

"I need you to hold me,
    mother a child,
I need your calming charm,
    when I am wild."

"I need you to share daily,
    happiness and gain,
I need you to smother away,
    an aching pain."

"I need you when life's day
    is growing dark,
to lighten the way with your
    wisdom and spark."

"I need your tenderness when
    everything seems grim,
to fulfill my goal in life,
    fill it to the brim."

"I need you more and more,
    as time passes by,
you are my companion, my friend,
    my life, my ally."

"Emptiness"

"Here I am meditating deeply,
    staring at the ceiling,
with my baby vacationing,
    I have that empty feeling."

"A feeling of emptiness each
    day and every night,
counting every single hour till,
    she's back within my sight."

"Time continues to pass away,
    minute by minute,
you try hard to concentrate,
    your mind isn't in it."

"That total incompleteness of
    being so far apart,
torments the peace of mind,
    tortures the lonely heart."

"You yearn for that moment of
    being together again,
but until that moment arrives,
    you visit memory lane."

"You recall the tender moments,
    together you shared,
those moments of tender passion,
    with emotions un-spared."

"When your love finally returns,
    the body tingles a chime,
with a song in your heart that
    will last a lifetime."

"The two of us reunited now,
    love has been strong,
that time spent separately, has
    been entirely too long."

"Income Tax"

"Hey! All you good people, it's
    that time of year,
for income and deductions,
    taxation time is here."

"Fix yourself a drink, sit back,
    and try to relax,
to figure out that yearly,
    dreadful income tax."

"With the proper concentration,
    and a little luck,
you'll remember another item,
    you've forgotten to deduct."

"Just how much did I earn,
    what does 'Uncle' get,
did I include everything,
    what did I forget?"

"It's figure and re-figure,
    add, and subtract,
for this ole document must,
    be legible and exact."

"It's that one day of the year,
    one does not boast,
about all those earnings,
    he or she has grossed."

"Riding on a Cloud"

"My daughter and I happily sit,
    riding on a cloud,
happy as a meadow lark,
    singing just as loud."

"Cruising 600 miles per hour,
    at thirty thousand feet,
overlooking the surface below,
    all blocked and very neat."

"Headed North-Easterly toward
    the Virginia coast,
that's God's territory which,
    I love the most."

"With my lovely young daughter,
    traveling hand-in-hand,
a nice visit with Grandma,
    revisiting my native land."

"With a song on my lips,
    love in my heart,
brings a tear to my eye,
    from the very start."

"Those old memories still linger,
    they're in the past,
the future's upon us now and
    moving along so fast."

"So I must value this and every day,
    as I do the rest,
to live life to the fullest, and
    give it my best."

"My Love"

"Heart of solid gold, I
    see that glaze,
eyes the deepest of blue,
    hair of blaze."

"That sweet warm kiss,
    longing caress,
calms my troubled heart,
    bringing happiness."

"Happy, lively and content,
    I'll always be,
if you are always there,
    to comfort me."

"So come to me dear, when
    you hear my call,
you are my life, my love,
    you are my all."

"Loving you always, in
    sadness and laughter,
to love you now, and
    life ever after."

"Doing Your Best"

"Pushing yourself at practice,
  day after day,
getting yourself prepared, in
  every possible way."

"Taking those vitamins, running
  that extra lap,
doing it over and over till
  it becomes a snap."

"Concentrating on the body as
  well as the mind,
both must work together, or
  you're left behind."

"Using that inner knowledge,
  as that added feed,
to achieve total power and
  that burst of speed."

"Extensive exercise and practice,
  is like a final test,
neither is much good unless it's
  your very, very, best."

"With mind and body equally,
  and totally trained.
That trophy at the finish line.
  Is much easier attained."

"You must be in the best shape,
    mind, body, and soul,
it gives you that added edge,
    in achieving that goal."

"Your time, effort, and energy,
    just isn't well spent,
if when you finally give, it's
    only fifty percent."

"My Life's Portrait"

"If you were to paint a
    portrait of my life,
you'd be painting color,
    with a little strife."

"Beyond the darkened clouds,
    came the sun so bright,
which colored my life so
    pure and pearly white."

"The sun shone brightly,
    every time it rained,
my heart weighing heavily for
    the love I had gained."

"Flowers forever in bloom,
    grass always green,
such a marvelous life, I
    had never seen."

"The moon so round and full,
    radiant in the night,
billions of sparkling stars,
    glistening so bright."

"Sharing the good times,
    along with the bad,
I was like a king on a throne,
    best life I ever had."

"You can visualize my portrait,
    of love and finesse,
a picture of rare beauty, and
    everlasting happiness."

"The Mystery of Life"

"Have you ever wondered about
    the mystery of life,
a human being can be
    conceived by your wife?"

"Feeding through her body,
    baby starts to form,
secure in its surroundings,
    safe from all harm."

"Nine months you wonder,
    nine months she'll bear,
human life within her through,
    tender love and care."

"The final moment arrives,
    be it boy or girl,
you wish it healthy,
    your head's in a whirl."

"With heart in your throat
    you wait and you pace,
time stands totally still,
    the outcome one must face."

"Prayers are finally answered,
    I don't mean maybe,
when they wheel you in, . . .
    a healthy new baby."

"So you pray to God above,
    you hope he hears,
the pouring of your heart,
    the everlasting cheers"

"Aircraft Guard"

"My rifle on my shoulder,
    I walked the pace,
I checked my aircraft and
    looked into space."

"I gazed into the clouds,
    so pure and white,
a jet flew swiftly overhead,
    then out of sight."

"The sun was slowly setting,
    but still so very bright,
a hour went speedily by,
    and it's almost night."

"Darkness slowly creeping in,
    day is growing old,
the moon is taking over,
    big, bright and bold."

"Now it's almost midnight,
    I am proud to say,
have just been relieved and
    I'm well on my way."

"Eight hours of guarding
    I had to stand,
when it was all over,
    sitting was a demand."

"Hand-in-Hand"

"Walking along hand-in-hand,
    strolling along the beach,
watching the waves caressing the
    shore within its reach."

"A shiny sea shell spaced,
    one here and there,
kids playing so happily,
    without a single care."

"A ship fading in the distance,
    heading toward open sea,
smaller boats much closer,
    on a fishing spree."

"Beaches of sugar-like sand,
    caressing the bay,
rippling tides changing everything
    during sun's bright day."

"Small scattered sand bars slowly,
    covered by the tide,
with each incoming wave, more
    shore begins to hide."

"Soon it's high tide and water covers
    most all the beach,
it's Mother Nature saying, you're
    now within my reach."

"Be a Buddy"

"You think anyone can be a
       daddy to a child,
but try being a buddy for
       just a little while."

"A friend to joke and play.
       A person to share,
a buddy to sit and listen,
       a father to care."

"Two partners sticking together
       through thick and thin,
compassion for one another,
       and love within."

"A love so pure and tender,
       lasting and strong,
always sticking together,
       singing a song."

"Showing that you really care,
       no ordering around,
creating that growing smile,
       diminishing that frown."

"By doing it together and
       completing those aims,
sharing those tender moments as
       well as the games."

"Feed on each other's friendship
       to the very end,
you will enjoy being a buddy,
       and not just a friend."

"Time Flies"

"The years quickly passing,
    no time for the past,
the planning for the future
    and hoping you'll last."

"With the kids in school, you
    give them the best,
soon they'll be gone then
    plenty time for rest."

"Children grow so fast today,
    you tend to shudder,
the butterflies you are feeling,
    begin to stir and flutter."

"Just where has time gone,
    surely I was there,
the aging of each single day,
    was given great care?"

"Time has really flown, but
    am I any bolder,
I don't feel any smarter, but
    do feel a bit older."

"The Girl I Met"

"Met a girl the other day that
    was quite a cutie,
had tantalizing blue eyes,
    charming little beauty."

"Red was her pretty long hair,
    a cute little nose,
skin so soft and delicate like
    petals of a shedding rose."

"She walked with such grace,
    holding head up high,
you could see the fellows,
    giving forth that sigh."

"A sigh not of passion as
    you'd sometimes fear,
but that of strong yearning to
    have a girl so dear."

"That marvelous beauty came
    from Mother Nature's skill,
it was done so tenderly and of
    her own free will."

"So always stay beautiful babe,
    and forever beware,
of fellows such as me, who
    always stop and stare."

"Freedom"

"Bad feelings of yester-year,
    when things you begun,
now a feeling of total relief,
    the emotion of having won."

"You look back with a-vision of
    dear ole yester-year,
you've made your decisions,
    and free of any fear."

"You journey yourself back in time,
    to years in the past,
now a sign of total relief,
    'cause you're free at last."

"Your lasting patience tested, to
    the fullest extent,
but now you're totally free,
    full of content."

"Free from the past mistakes,
    once you had made,
now a new chance for life,
    a future not afraid."

"Once a slave to conscience,
    but now I am free, so
now I'll enjoy my life,
    a little more tenderly."

"Isn't life wonderful when
    it's going your way,
today is, ah, so different,
    than it was yesterday."

"Death's Course"

"Death captures all creatures
        taking young and old,
once it has taken its course, a
        never ending strong hold."

"Death moves about us daily,
        in so many ways,
you can learn to accept it,
        or stay in a haze."

"The heart ceases to beat,
        blood runs cold,
there's no turning back,
        death takes its toll."

"When it finally takes over,
        your very last breath,
you've just been introduced
        to the kiss of death."

"Death can be joyous,
        it can be sad,
can be totally good,
        or be very, very bad."

"Every one's path in life,
        no matter where it ends,
leads to that lasting trail
        the termination begins."

"Death is mandatory at the
        end of that trail,
the mind must be ready before
        the soul goes stale."

"Creator of life and death,
    equally divine,
it's the preparation beforehand,
    and the frame of mind."

"Prepare yourself for the end,
    before you depart,
give your soul to GOD and
    he'll save your heart."

"That final tally figured,
    at the going rate,
it's nice to know when you've
    entered the 'Pearly Gate.' "

"Changes"

"A lot of drastic changes,
    this past year,
so I think I'll relax, and
    have me a beer."

"A lot of good simple things,
    which changed my life,
overcoming a deep hurt,
    a lot of strife."

"A feeling that your sanity is
    now on the brink,
you prepare yourself just a
    little stronger drink."

"Many things happened daily, as
    if it were fate,
some of them very bad,
    other ones great."

"Things that you didn't control
    which really exploded,
think I'll have another drink,
    maybe even get loaded."

"A Lot of extreme difficulties,
    happened in my mind,
which changed my attitude,
    left the rest behind."

"Just a little mixed up and,
    what life to choose,
I think everything will clear up,
    Just a little more booze."

"True Love"

"Life without true love,
    has no definite meaning,
like a child's fantasy,
    fun of day-dreaming."

"Sincere love is like a treasure,
    very often sought,
misused and misled,
    but never bought."

"A false love is bought and sold,
    often in a lifetime,
but true love survives,
    the bells will chime."

"Once in a lifetime for both,
    the young and old,
true love is forever sought,
    to share, to hold."

"When that deep feeling exists,
    in heart and mind,
becomes a truer lasting love,
    so special to find."

"Sex is driving function,
    love is a thriving emotion,
physical love a desire, . . .
    mental love a devotion."

"A fiery passion lasts but,
   a moment of endeavor,
while true love plus passion,
   lasts forever and ever."

"Mental love does excite that
   physical driving crave,
mold the two desires together,
   both will be your slave."

"A New Home"

"I watched an animal captured,
  tranquilized, and caged,
when it awoke it was so
  upset and enraged."

"In such a strange habitat,
  looking for a home,
a place to eat and sleep,
  a place to roam."

"A brand new home and yet
  a strange environment,
a simple habitation forever
  for its retirement."

"With a hairy like face, it
  inspected every corner,
looking all about with hate,
  saying, I'm a goner."

"All of a sudden the young
  ape was not alone.
Just out of no-where sprang
  a mate to condone."

"Living in a restricted cage,
  surviving was his motto,
that hairy little black ape.
  We called him Otto."

"To him this strange home
  was ah! so new,
he called it a new home,
  we called it a zoo."

"Our New Home"

"Dear happy little house, you
    are really very small,
big enough for love,
    two people having a ball."

"Each room carefully decorated,
    with tender love and care,
every picture precisely placed,
    one here . . . another there."

"Plenty of fresh country air,
    watching a morning sun,
a cup of coffee on the patio,
    can be a lot of fun."

"Oh! How great it is, watching
    the summer breeze,
covering the earth with warmness,
    swaying the tall green trees."

"Oh! How too soon an individual,
    tends to forget,
living in the country was great,
    not a single regret."

"So, here I am my friends,
    full of love and content,
remembering all the times,
    together we spent."

"We really do love you house,
    that, we do condone,
please shelter and protect us,
    a house turned into a home."

"Introduction to Birth"

"Little boy or little girl I
    did not favor,
all I ever wanted was
    avoiding that labor."

"Holding your hand tightly
    I watched you scream,
it was so much like just
    another bad dream."

"Laboring steadily and hard,
    that lasting pain,
me feeling a little worried,
    and you in a strain."

"Just all of a sudden there's a
    flash of relief,
the little toddler baby was here,
    mystified all belief."

"I ran swiftly for the doctor,
    they came quickly,
they ran me out of the room,
    I was feeling sickly."

"Soon everything's O.K.,
    my nerves calmed down,
out wheeled a little baby girl in
    her hospital gown."

"She was so beautiful, a
    seven-pound little girl,
that was one rainy night I
    stayed in a whirl."

"Snow in the Night"

"The tranquility of darkness,
    creeping over the city,
dusk fading into the shadows,
    with dignity and pity."

"Snowflakes are slowly falling on
    the frost bitten ground,
this night is going slowly,
    silence is all around."

"Calmness is the wind and brisk
    is the winter air,
large flakes now falling rapidly,
    without a single care."

"A gigantic milky blanket of
    sparkling white,
has covered the spacious earth
    so beautiful and bright."

"The leafless drooping trees
    stood coated and pale,
branches of pearly white and
    their shadows frail."

"Tomorrow the sun will shine,
    melting the pearly snow,
disappearing so rapidly,
    turning into a liquid flow."

"The scene now is over,
    it's time to depart,
so please accept this marvel,
    a true work of art."

"Conclusion"

"Just where do you go, or
    what do you do,
is life getting you down,
    depressing, or blue?"

"Where does an individual's
    obligation end,
deeply burying the past,
    seeking happiness again?"

"Many a beautiful sunset has
    come and past,
but your mind has told you, it
    just wouldn't last."

"Just how do you explain, or
    tell your child, . . .
Daddy just won't be around
    for a little while?"

"That deep loving attachment
    cannot be revealing,
if you have lost all of the,
    feel of feeling."

"Feelings from the heart is
    what it's all about,
you've either got it or
    you are left without."

"If your heart won't respond
    to a single reflex,
is like a Chinese torture,
    placing a 'Hex on sex.' "

"Lonely for You"

"With my pen in hand,
    I'll try to express,
my loneliness for you,
    using a little finesse."

"We have been apart but
    a very few days,
I miss you so terribly,
    let me count the ways."

"I miss your tenderness,
    the sexy way you walk,
giving a little smile,
    expressive way you talk."

"I miss that tender kiss
    we share every night,
I miss our bodies touching,
    way you hold me tight."

"I miss that tender sparkle
    gleam in your eye,
I miss the companionship that
    makes a friendship tie."

"I miss the home environment,
    we share daily together,
the working side by side,
    in all kinds of weather."

"But now that uneasy ill feeling,
    I'll discard tomorrow,
My lovely sweetheart arrives,
    Happiness replaces sorrow."

146

"Reflections"

"There once was a little boy dressed in
    a grown man's suit,
trying to figure out the entire world,
    analyzing every dispute."

"Looking into the frameless mirror
    viewing the past,
trying to figure the future and
    how it can last."

"Looking within vivid reflections,
    researching daily life,
viewing the joyful happy times,
    forgetting the strife."

"That face in that tarnished mirror
    has stayed the same,
the little boy has fully grown,
    shedding his shame."

"Facing the mighty world on
    a collision course,
analyzing the past failures and
    seeking their source."

"Setting pleasant new goals,
    a new destination,
Life's journey straight ahead,
    with great anticipation."

"The future now ahead of me,
    moving so very fast,
the mirror is my mental vision,
    of my distant past."

"Life's Hourglass"

"All engrossed in life,
  as an older lass,
I slowly watched sand sift,
  through Life's Hourglass."

"When life was confusing,
  like Helta Skelta,
you took me in your life, you
  gave me shelter."

"I owe to you dear so
  very, very much,
when I was stumbling along.
  You were my crutch."

"You loved me with tenderness,
  really cared for me,
you did it with pure grace
  and a gentle dignity."

"Taking sufficient time to
  unconfuse my life,
you loved me so dearly,
  within my strife."

"I morally owe my conscience,
  a simple guarantee,
unscramble my troubled life,
  regain my sanity."

"I respectfully owe to myself,
  an attempt to find,
what I want out of life,
  and peace of mind."

"Say It with a Flower"

"Say how you really feel
    hour after hour,
say it with the deepest feeling,
    give a pretty flower."

"Say it with pretty flowers,
    say it with love,
tell her, 'It's really you,
    I'm thinking of.' "

"A long-stemmed rose to
    show you still care,
to show that someone, the
    feeling is still there."

"A simple white carnation.
    A tulip or two,
a colorful way of saying,
    I still care for you."

"Just say I love you so,
    do it with a flower,
the love within you will bloom,
    hour after hour."

"That lasting heavenly fragrance
    superseded by beauty,
a simple little delicate flower
    just doing its duty."

"Smiling at a lovely flower in
    a heart warming way,
what a beautiful gesture and
    you've just made my day."

"Thanksgiving"

"Thanksgiving is much more than
    a historical fable,
or a delicious turkey just
    sitting on the table."

"Thanksgiving is much more than
    fancy decorated meals,
it's really the deep thoughtful thanks
    the heart really feels."

"A feast carefully prepared with
    tender love and care,
a symbol of family and friendship,
    closeness to share."

"Expressing the traditions our
    ancestors journeyed through,
with stress and hardships overcome,
    faith in mankind coming true."

"What's so very special today,
    about a thanksgiving,
it's giving your thanks for,
    just everyday living."

"My Lasting Love"

"If one could measure distance,
    to the clouds above,
would prove much smaller,
    than my lasting love."

"Millions of stars glowing in
    a star-lit night,
could not possibly match,
    our love so bright."

"My lasting love for you is
    somewhat like a flower,
nourished day by day tenderly,
    growing by the hour."

"Sparkling ripples of a cool
    mountain spring,
cannot surpass this feeling,
    my heart's rippling."

"So fondly in love with you,
    I'll always be,
you are my deepest desire,
    my destiny."

"Our World"

"If in this troubled old world,
    loved as you and I,
would change the nation,
    all hate would die."

"If all of us made friends,
    through fun and labor,
wars being no longer but
    loving thy neighbor."

"We are so close together
    yet so far away,
our love never fading till
    our dying day."

"We are in a special world
    of our very own,
a world of love that has,
    just grown and grown."

"We must have each other
    I know it is true,
but till that day arrives,
    I'll always be blue."

"Drifting"

"Ever just sit back in
    your easy chair,
drift into a world which,
    really wasn't there?"

"No stubbornly arguments,
    no sign of war,
no trace of prejudices,
    no sign of living poor."

"Taxes are just unheard of,
    bills are people's names,
children playing together,
    their silly little games."

"If this world does exist,
    someday we'll find,
this haven we're looking for,
    and peace of mind."

"A world of precious beauty,
    kindness, and love,
it must be 'Heaven' I've
    been thinking of."

"Love Me"

"Love me with your eyes.
    Love me with your heart,
love me now and forever,
    nevermore to part."

"Love me all the day,
    love me all night,
love me now and forever,
    it's my delight."

"Love me in the Spring,
    love me in the Fall,
love me now and forever,
    love me most of all."

"Love me in the scorching sun,
    love me in the rain,
love me now and forever,
    but love not in vain."

"Love me when I'm sad,
    love me in laughter,
love me now and forever,
    and life ever after."

"Mark of Beauty"

"The radiant beauty of those
    tantalizing eyes,
sparked with glamour as did
    the curves of her size."

"She walked with that poise,
    the grace of a queen,
was such a lovely beauty,
    I had ever seen."

"Silk was her glowing complexion,
    soft was her skin,
reminding me of the beautiful,
    world that we are in."

"All the right things in all
    the right places,
causing minds to wonder,
    hearts to the races."

"Such a lovely, beautiful creature,
    a fine work of art,
would haunt any sane man,
    tear his mind apart."

"Arguing"

"Whether you think you're wrong or
    think you are right,
it's just so totally senseless, to
    continue to fight."

"I can easily remember yesterday,
    a time of bliss,
but didn't ever suspect,
    things ending like this."

"When you have had your
    back against the wall,
you call, 'time out,' and
    use up a pressure call."

"Realizing all the mistakes,
    you have made,—
shows how that lasting love,
    surely did fade."

"One can change or alter,
    a beautiful work of art,
impossible to change feelings,
    of a broken down heart."

"After long deep thoughts, and
    careful consideration,
I have decided to spend my life,
    in total moderation."

"Three Loves"

"Normally three women in
    a young man's life,
can bring total misery,
    a lot of strife."

"In my particular case,
    I love all three,
each love a little different,
    but most tenderly."

"One's a mother's tender love
    shared from birth,
to cherish her always till
    the end of earth."

"A precious little daughter to
    love and to hold,
to grow into maturity,
    watch grandkids grow old."

"A passionate loving woman,
    moments you cherish,
a partnership forever but
    daily you nourish."

"So now you can see why
    I really care,
my most special three loves,
    each so pure and rare."

"First Smile"

"When used to crying just
    like a Cherokee,
a pretty little smile, . . .
    you'll long to see."

"An occasional fierce cry,
    sometimes being vile,
but what's more beautiful
    than baby's first smile?"

"A smile that warms you
    deep down inside,
a wonderful deep feeling,
    baby is your pride."

"Baby's tender little smile,
    showing you she's content,
thanking you for everything
    and the time you've spent."

"A gooey little smile is
    baby's only way,
thanking you for caring so,
    every single day."

"That baby's first smile,
    your lasting treasure,
so when she smiles at you, . . .
    it's her pleasure."

"A Special Day"

"Today, of all joyful days,
    a very special day,
should be cherished tenderly
    in every possible way."

"A lot has happened through
    all kinds of weather,
survived the stormy-seas,
    we did it together."

"Time quickly journeys onward,
    this year has past,
the birth of a new season,
    but the memories last."

"A delightful anniversary,
    a contented wife,
a family in harmony,
    an active life."

"So we celebrate this day,
    quiet dinner for two,
a sip of sparkling wine,
    another year to re-new."

"When I think about yesteryear,
    memories I do borrow,
but I look upon today as the
    doorway of tomorrow."

"Mother's Lullaby"

"Rock a bye little baby,
    your mommy is tired,
rock a bye, little baby,
    your daddy expired."

"When your heart breaks,
    you yell and you cry,
and mommy comes running
    to see if you're dry."

"She gives you your milk
    and sings you a song,
and hope you are sleepy
    and won't take long."

"Lay your head down and
    shut those blue eyes,
soon you'll be up and running,
    just before sunrise."

"Rock a bye little baby,
    we hope you won't weep,
rock a bye little baby,
    your daddy needs sleep."

"Please go to sleep now,
    give us a break,
please go to sleep now, . . .
    for goodness sake."

"Happy Anniversary"

"Another wonderful year
    gone by so fast,
each one so special,
    better than the last."

"In sickness and in health,
    through thick and thin,
working together as a team,
    we're sure to win."

"The times we shared together,
    both good and bad,
one tolerating the other,
    when upset or mad."

"A fifty-fifty proposition
    may not always be,
so at those critical times,
    treat one tenderly."

"Blissful, beautiful moments,
    sincere and ever true,
but remembering always, . . .
    it always takes two."

"So happy anniversary dear,
    for words cannot express,
my undying love for you and
    everlasting happiness."

"Outer Space"

"What is this thing called
      the human race,
a fight to totally conquer
      the outer space?

"Who will triumph and
      who will lose,
this is a lasting battle
      we seem to choose?"

"All want to be first so
      space is under attack,
getting there doesn't bother me,
      it's getting us back."

"The money we have spent to
      launch and to test,
wanting to be the first and
      being the best."

"We test our powerful rockets,
      improvements we adjust,
all mankind working together.
      Our goal becomes a must."

"It's a race to the finish to
      reach the moon,
I hope it's the United States
      and hope it's soon."

"Where Am I?"

"In the middle of an island,
    far out at sea,
nine thousand miles from you,
    where can I be?"

"I know it isn't Hawaii nor
    even scenic Japan,
just what place is this,
    such a secluded land?"

"It's thirty-five miles long,
    four to eight miles wide,
coconut palm trees all over,
    I still can't decide."

"The climate is awful hot,
    heat makes you lazy,
where in the world am I,
    It's driving me crazy?"

"I thought and thought and
    arrived this conclusion,
it's either Guam or Hell
    surely not an illusion."

"Both mean the same thing and
    are four letter words,
'tis our slang expression, . . .
    'It's strictly for the birds.' "

"Love Just Doesn't Live Here Anymore"

"If you visualize your life
    a nerve-racking bore,
and you just don't care
    who walks through the door," . . . then

"<u>Love just doesn't live here anymore.</u>"

"If you're cruising on a ship,
    always looking for shore,
and you feel the distance,
    which you can't take anymore," . . . then

"<u>Love just doesn't live here anymore.</u>"

"When the riches of your life
    tend to make you poor,
and that favorite woman
    looks better next door," . . . then

"<u>Love just doesn't live here anymore.</u>"

"When the woman you live with is
    not the one you adore,
feeling like the bull in a ring,
    and, not the matador," . . . then

"<u>Love just doesn't live here anymore.</u>"

"When that 'ship' coming in
    seems to lose an oar,
and you sit amid wonder just
    what you're waiting for," . . . then

"<u>Love just doesn't live here anymore.</u>"

"When the tree of life you,
    tend to completely ignore
and instead of one precious love—
    you'd rather be with four," . . . then

"<u>Love just doesn't live here anymore.</u>"

"When you feel life's end near and
    friends around you, you deplore,
then I guess its really true,
    just as I said before," . . . I know

"<u>Love just doesn't live here anymore.</u>"

"My Suit of Hearts"

"Ace of Hearts" . . . "is number one and you're the one for me."

"Two of Hearts" . . . "is for two hearts we tied together."

"Three of Hearts" . . . "three wonderful children we love and cherish."

"Four of Hearts" . . . "four seasons of the year we share together."

"Five of Hearts" . . . "the five in our family of togetherness."

"Six of Hearts" . . . "is for the six years we have shared together."

"Seven of Hearts" . . . "number of days in the week we share our love."

"Eight of Hearts" . . . "hours in the day my dreams of you."

"Nine of Hearts" . . . "number of decades we will share together."

"Ten of Hearts" . . . "ten thousand words cannot express my love for you."

"Jack of Hearts" . . . "the one who first introduced us."

"Queen of Hearts" . . . "you're the queen of my heart."

"King of Hearts" . . . "is the way you always make me feel."

"The Traveler"

"Thinking the travel agent
    wasn't very bright,
I decided to take vacation,
    so planned taking a flight."

"I decided on a schedule,
    paid the bargain fare.
Through the security to gate twenty one,
    the plane already there."

"The boarding announcement
    so loud and so clear,
I boarded my flight,
    Take-off was near."

"I searched for my seat number,
    someone already there,
so I picked another one,
    I didn't really care."

"The aircraft door shut,
    engines started roaring,
I was totally relaxed,
    found myself snoring."

"A hour long flight,
    a hour long nap,
why did the hostess lay,
    a napkin in my lap?"

"I called to the hostess.
    'Something's not right,'
we've been airborne too long.
    It's not a meal flight.' "

"We're headed where?
    I said in a strain,
how was I able to board,
    the wrong blasted plane?"

"The hostess said to me,
    don't be so nervous,
just sit back and relax,
    enjoy the ultra service."

"When I get back home,
    I'm talking to someone,
about that 'HOLY TERROR'
    of gate twenty-one."

"A Wintry Eve"

"On a brisk wintry eve I
    decided to burn a log,
as a sure starter I used
    an old catalog."

"Placing the split logs
    neatly on the grate,
just one match was all it
    took to generate."

"The eve was cool and crisp,
    early in the night,
the fire burned briskly
    with pure delight."

"Flames encircled the logs
    trying to devour,
lying there so helplessly,
    lasting for an hour."

"The warm air felt good as it
    caressed my face,
sending a warm sensation
    of warm embrace."

"The fireplace blazed with
    a radiant glow,
escaping within the chimney,
    trying to overthrow."

"Yellow streaks of fiery heat
    with a reddish tip,
converted the logs into ashes,
    destroying my workmanship."

"I sensed myself dropping off
	into a staring gaze,
I was being hypnotized by
	the burning blaze."

"It had taken control of my mind,
	cast me into a fog,
the flame diminished and I awoke,
	to find another log."

"Recalling My Youth"

"As I recap those youthful days,
    those teenage years,
brought me many hardships,
    a lot of tears."

"Looking for leadership and guidance,
    finding myself in strife,
my life as a simple farm boy wasn't
    such a happy life."

"Trying to do all the right things
    with two left feet,
growing slowly into manhood and
    learning to be neat."

"Doing my routine daily chores,
    just after school,
trying to milk old 'Betsy,'
    without a stool."

"Learning so many difficult things, as
    you worked all day,
and for an awkward little boy,
    it's the hardest way."

"Plowing land with an old tractor,
    spike-wheeled and unique,
all day getting the job done,
    with that old antique."

"Feeding those restless greedy hogs,
    repairing a fence,
trying to become a man plus
    build my confidence."

"The many things that I did learn,
    as a growing boy,
went with me into manhood,
    knowledge I did employ."

"So as I look backward at that,
    little boy on a farm,
I smile very softly because,
    I weathered the storm."

"Memories of Yesterday"

"In looking for lasting memories,
    in life's hide-a-way,
I recalled a special evening,
    tokens of yesterday."

"Cocktails just for two in a
    secluded place,
two hearts reunited,
    a warm embrace."

"An atmosphere of soft music,
    dinner by candlelight,
toasting cheers to each other
    well into the night."

"Two hungry bodies molded into
    a time of passion,
one trying to please the other,
    forgetting the fashion."

"Awakening relaxed and content, in
    each other's charms,
bodies in complete fulfillment,
    locked in each other's arms."

"A beautiful tender evening,
    I'll never forget,
such an everlasting memory,
    I'll never regret."

"Tranquility"

"You can feel the tranquility of
    dawn's morning wake,
when a cloud of fog raises from
    resting on a lake."

"Birds with tiny heads bowed,
    winged against their breast,
the morning dew fades as they
    awaken in their nests."

"The morning dew diminishes,
    at dawn's early light,
the sun takes over and gives
    the evergreens delight."

"The earth and its inhabitants,
    start the day at birth,
life slowly comes alive as
    the sun warms the earth."

"A huge fish splashes breaking
    dawn's peaceful trend,
searching for food eagerly,
    just around a bend."

"Gulls searching for fish,
    fish searching for food,
creatures seeking the survival,
    both masterful and crude."

"A rippling wave drifting gracefully
    toward the distant shore,
a fisherman enjoying his boat,
    alternating his oar."

"What a relaxing deep feeling,
     within my soul,
when that tranquil sensation,
     takes total control."

"Through my vision of tranquility,
     I observe all these things,
is my escape from reality, and
     what my writing brings."

"Storm Rolling In"

"As I lay there pondering,
    awaiting the storm,
listening to the thunder, and
    watching clouds take form."

"The wind blew swiftly with,
    a powering breeze,
blowing curtains from windows,
    swaying the trees."

"First the lightening and thunder,
    then single drops of rain,
suddenly a cloud burst that,
    saturated the earth's terrain."

"Streaks of lightning bolts,
    rippling across the sky,
dividing portions of gray as
    Heaven continued to cry."

"Soon the thunder stooped,
    the lightning didn't last,
the down pouring rain diminished,
    now a storm in the past."

"Storms to me are fascinating,
    even a mystery,
this storm now a tender moment,
    now a part of history."

"Life's Crossroads"

"Standing at life's crossroad knowing,
    not which way to go,
tired of daily trials and tribulations,
    and putting on a show."

"In analyzing my tangled life,
    I gave it my best,
something was just missing,
    I failed the test."

"I gave up my many assets,
    including my family,
to search out my goal in life,
    my individuality."

"With so many paths in the road,
    you select just one,
looking for that peace within,
    in life's garrison."

"There's many detours on life's highway,
    each a different direction,
one must know what turn to make,
    at life's intersection."

"I know I've made wrong turns,
    even run out of road,
but with the guidance of God above,
    will help carry my load."

"Walls"

"Recalling those tender moments,
    within these walls,
I can remember building shelves,
    painting the halls."

"Those questionable goals normally,
    I'd never attempt,
but knowing the needs of my family,
    I put nothing exempt."

"A lot of hard work deep within,
    some you just can't see,
the work, sweat and love,
    I did so willingly."

"If these walls could speak out,
    they'd graciously sing,
a tender song of work and love,
    through life's laboring."

"There's abundance of love and tears,
    stored within these walls,
through the many daily hardships,
    faced many downfalls."

"One day in this precious life,
    I'll look back and see,
how those walls in my jumbled life,
    loved and protected me."

"Tempers Flare"

"When two tempers flare up,
    as yours and mine,
vicious words generously cast,
    far from being kind."

"Things have happened so quickly,
    in both our pasts,
sent us in opposite directions and
    I viewed the forecast."

"I value our close friendship,
    but now I must part,
our tempers each a masterpiece
    and a fine show of art."

"When two minds tangle so,
    one must win,
our friendship I won't sacrifice,
    so I'll take it on the chin."

"So I bid thee farewell friend,
    our paths did cross,
this tender friendship of ours,
    I'll not double cross."

"One day as you journey back,
    just ponder the past,
I hope you can smile and say,
    we made the friendship last."

"Inflation"

"No predictions are ever,
    precisely exact,
but inflation is truly here,
    that's a proven fact."

"Airlines struggling to stay,
    within the black,
no relief in sight to
    take up the slack."

"These times are really bad,
    may even get worse,
positive thinking is essential,
    bad ones you disperse."

"By pinching the feeble penny,
    stretching the dollar,
is still not simply enough to
    educate the scholar."

"Everyone striving desperately,
    to make ends meet,
determined to survive,
    avoiding defeat."

"It's hard to be patriotic or
    remember a fable,
when you are fighting hard to
    keep food on the table."

"Things have to change soon,
    hopefully for the best,
then you can smile and say,
    "I've passed the test."

"So hang in there folks, be tough,
    we've got to stay free,
it's our duty, our life,
    our destiny."

"The Double Within"

"Who are these identical twins,
    within your tattered soul,
one tender and loving,
    the other hard and cold?"

"It's like two desperate people,
    both wanting to shout,
each demanding individuality,
    trying to get out."

"One kind and generous with,
    love and understanding,
the other mad and vicious,
    totally demanding."

"One thrives on the sting of a
    wounded dying bee,
the other consumes the honey,
    so pure, sweet, and tenderly."

"One is shrewd, selfish, devious,
    just always cruel,
challenging the world daily in
    an everlasting duel."

"One is a loving individual striving
    to overcome daily strife,
casting away the negative traits,
    getting the best out of life."

"Life must be put in harmony,
    control that dual personality,
the good will overcome evil,
    giving individuality."

"Treat your fellow man as
     you would be treated,
and the devil within you will
     be totally defeated."

"All have positive traits,
     negative ones as well,
by placing both in retrospect,
     strife submits farewell."

"The Turmoil Within"

"I can see the pain and hurt within
    those saddened eyes,
I can see the turmoil created by
    your painted lies."

"Lies that camouflage the truth
    to lessen the pain,
not intending to hurt anyone,
    soothing a troubled brain."

"I see a hurt little girl trying so
    desperately to get out,
I see a grown woman totally confused,
    just full of doubt."

"Two compelling voices within One soul,
    one kind and true,
the other troubled and struggling,
    finding life in a stew."

"A false picture of fantasy to
    ease a growing pain,
hoping that your individuality
    soon to regain."

"Wondering about yourself but
    striving for peace within,
not knowing just how to achieve it,
    you relying on a friend."

"Unless one can totally separate these
    churned emotions in one's self,
will be a life entirely of turmoil,
    feelings bottled on a shelf."

"Friends can help you take those
    feelings off that shelf,
opening your heart to total truth,
    understanding the inner self."

"Just knowing yourself completely will
    open life's door,
to that total peace within you that
    you've been striving for."

"Dream Come True"

"She walked towards me with grace,
    dignity and pride,
I could see the electricity, in
    her womanly stride."

"That life-giving warmth of an
    affectionate smile,
proud of her youthful body,
    clothed in flavored style."

"She spoke with a joyful expression,
    through ruby red lips,
her features poised and full with a
    slight swing of the hips."

"As I gazed deep into those piercing,
    tantalizing eyes,
I became speechless, entranced,
    totally mesmerized."

"I was torn between disbelief,
    crave and desire,
I could feel that deep burning,
    setting my heart afire."

"She confirmed my dreams of a
    perfect work of art,
she's now a vivid reality,
    upset my apple cart."

"Inner Peace Within"

"I hope one day you'll awake to find,
    a broken heart mended,
all that turmoil deep within you,
    will have finally ended."

"You will see different shades of blue
    in a heavenly sky,
instead of that storm deep within you,
    that made you cry."

"You will see and enjoy Mother Nature
    at her very best,
inner conflict within you gone, letting
    mind and body rest."

"You will look into the mirror and
    thank God you're alive,
then those Heavenly Angels of mercy
    will help you survive."

"Having finally achieved that precious goal,
    to live and, let live,
then you can confront your fellow man,
    reaping as you give."

"When you can look towards the future,
    storing the hardened past,
saving the best of those memories that
    thus far made you last."

"When you can face each single day,
    looking for the next,
your life is worth living because
    life's your daily text."

"All of this added up totals that
    inner peace within,
looking upon life and where you're going,
    not where you have been."

"Grandma"

"Five generations of family history,
    marks this special day,
a century of birthdays celebrated in
    a very personal way."

"One hundred years of wisdom with
    lot of credit due,
is a unique way of saying,
    Hi! Grandma, we love you."

"We will always love you, Grandma,
    till the end of time,
may this be your very special day,
    celebrating your prime."

"Autumn Leaves"

"With visions of a beautiful summer,
      coming to a close,
opens its mighty doors to Autumn,
      and what it might impose."

"Days growing much shorter with
      a coolness of night,
those who dread its swift arrival,
      shutter at its sight."

"The trees acting so restless,
      with an Autumn Wind,
leaves falling from their master,
      floating to journey's end."

"Trees stripped of their modest clothing
      when needing it most,
standing nude with honor and dignity,
      saluting an Autumn toast."

"A blanket of golden leaves made
      into a pillow of rust,
separated from their creator,
      into a bed of crust."

"Oh! Autumn leaves, Oh! Autumn leaves,
      you've met your quest,
you've truly earned your way
      into eternal rest."

"A combination of yellow, rust, and gold,
      you've converted the forest green,
into the most beautiful, masterpiece,
      I have ever seen."

"The Height of Depression"

"Oh! How deep the hurt is within,
    this battered soul,
everything in life looking grim,
    blood running cold."

"How could anyone cast such
    a tremendous blow,
when it's that someone that
    once inspired you so?"

"My life's long work is now,
    just an empty dream,
the hurt within my aching gut,
    cries a silent scream"

"My heartbeat pounding so rapidly,
    like drums of war,
I have truly enslaved myself,
    my own feelings I disbar."

"All my drive in life was,
    to constantly give,
now life an empty future with
    no reason to live."

"I've lost my individual pride,
    plus my goal in life,
I'll now die a total failure,
    engulfed in my strife."

"Life's Journey Forward"

"As my life journeys forward,
    into fascinations and dreams,
life itself becomes more challenging
    traveling through my teens."

"I know not what lies ahead, or,
    which path to take,
those paths of unfortunate prospects,
    decisions I must make."

"Sometimes that fork in the road,
    means no turning back,
but you climb swiftly out of it,
    using finesse and tact."

"The path in life's road is not smooth,
    there's obstacles along the way,
but if I'm really determined to make it,
    I'll truly find it some day."

"Summer Reminder"

"A welcomed Summer rain,
    cried heavenly tears of joy,
as they brushed against my brow,
    reminding me of a little boy."

"A little boy skipping gracefully
    in a carefree caressing rain,
soaked to the bone and uncaring,
    watching Mother Nature entertain."

"Feeding plants, animals, and mankind,
    with nourishing fruits of life,
realizing without it would bring,
    hardships, drought and strife."

"Carefree as a newborn babe,
    drops danced about the air,
full of grace and but control,
    with not a single care."

"Caressing the dry parched earth,
    with wetness of a heavy dew,
Mother Nature watering her garden,
    giving plant life anew."

"Thank you God, for those, . . .
    heavenly tears of joy,
that took me back into the past,
    to a young little boy."

"It Hurts"

"It hurts, observing a beautiful sunset,
    slowly meeting its doom,
sinking into the distant horizon,
    seduced by a lover's moon."

"It hurts, watching Mother Nature,
    sending a mild Summer rain,
cooling the dry parched earth,
    freeing its smoldering pain."

"It hurts, seeing sweethearts walking gracefully,
    hand-in-hand in the park,
engrossed in each other's warm embrace,
    happy as a lark."

"It hurts, feeling the passions of fire,
    deep within your soul,
dwindling only into powdery ashes,
    a flame gone cold."

"It hurts, thinking of a past gone by,
    your hopes and your dreams,
surpassed only by the painful silence
    of your inner screams."

"It hurts, knowing everything you've painted
    in this portrait of life,
has brought you unresting energies to
    overcome an artist's strife."

"It hurts, Oh! How it hurts, still life
    travels fast and strong,
hoping one day to find who you are,
    and where you belong."

"New Year's Eve"

"I was invited to my boss's party,
    New Year's Eve in eighty-three,
I felt like celebrating the end sending
    the year into history."

"Being introduced to everyone, I
    then walked toward you,
visions of a slender, shapely body,
    came fully within my view."

"Our penetrating eyes met as
    the introduction came,
seeing only the beautiful brown eyes,
    I almost missed your name."

"Pretty hair of a woven brown,
    with a tint of red,
speaking in a graceful manner,
    poise of a thoroughbred."

"Walking with dignity and pride,
    you generated such a heat,
that my heart fluttered a bit, . . .
    maybe missed a beat."

"We talked about likes and dislikes,
    as '83 came to an end,
having that magnetic personality,
    the stranger became a friend."

"Happy New Year brown eyes, . . .
    embrace and fiery lips net,
was a perfect introduction to '84,
    a memory I'll never forget."

"Brown Eyes"

"I'm sorry brown eyes that,
    I want you so much,
I just can't help myself,
    longing for your touch."

"How I long for our lips to touch
    in a fiery embrace,
I yearn for that fabulous feeling,
    that makes the heartbeat race."

"I want you so terribly much,
    to hold you in my arms,
to feel the warmth of your body,
    engrossed in your charms."

"If I had but one single wish,
    would be not wanting you so,
I then could face everyday reality,
    and I could let you go."

"The cards have been dealt so
    I'll play it to the end,
but I can not bring myself to be,
    just a casual friend."

"A Thank You Prayer"

"Thank you dear God, for
    giving me new life,
taking me hand in hand,
    overcoming my strife."

"When I was feeble and weak,
    you made me strong,
when I was down and depressed,
    you gave me song."

"When I was feeling bad,
    you cured my ills,
you paved the lighted path,
    flattening the hills."

"You gave me a loving mate
    to care for me,
a friend to love and cherish,
    loving tenderly."

"You were the solid rock,
    in my bed of sand,
you asked for nothing,
    giving a helping hand."

"You stuck by my side
    when I needed you so,
thank you again my Lord,
    it's truly you I owe."

"Poet's Release"

"Relaying my most inner thoughts,
    through writing a line,
alerting the entire world,
    sharing what's mine."

"Searching for the deepest thoughts,
    attempting to unwind,
seeking that a poet's total release
    of a silent mind."

"Analyzing the mind and soul,
    is what you will see,
casting out this inner sense,
    deep inside of me."

"What makes that determined drive,
    what makes me click,
what pushes me furiously onward,
    making the brain artistic?"

"Those tender precious thoughts,
    also my secret fears,
I see tender feelings withdrawn,
    and held back tears."

"I want a complete release of
    that secret desire,
setting mind and body totally free,
    that burns like fire."

"But as I transcribe my feelings,
    so ends the night,
putting mind, body, and soul to rest,
    so ends the fight."

"All these things released,
    deep down inside of me,
my feelings scribed on paper,
    are now let go free."

"Braniff Family"

"The old Braniff DFW family,
    is growing thin,
we've taken a severe beating,
    all on the chin."

"Employees scattered everywhere,
    North, East, South, & West,
but we did it so proudly,
    sticking out our chest."

"Who transfers to what city,
    what shift to choose,
I just don't know about this,
    I'm so confused!"

"I know things will pan out,
    everything back on track,
the family reunited, and
    getting our sanity back."

"Braniff is our future, our maker,
    it's our crutch,
let's all hang in there together,
    stay in touch."

"Braniff DFW is hanging on,
    the silent majority,
but the love for Braniff,
    has super seniority."

"Braniff, Oh! Braniff"

"Oh! Braniff, Oh! Braniff,
  where have you gone,
you've faded into the sunset,
  not to return at dawn?"

"Many happy fruitful years,
  dwindled into the past,
who'd ever, ever thought,
  this one's your last."

"You toiled, struggled, and fought,
  year after year,
built into the business world,
  a dedicated pioneer."

"The airline fight was fierce,
  trying to stay alive,
to win the travelers battle,
  plus family survive."

"So many stumbling blocks,
  along journey's way,
sights set on tomorrow,
  omitting ones today."

"Who'd ever believe a Braniff,
  that we all cherished,
now a moment of history
  among the perished."

"Braniff, oh! Braniff,
  we thought you'd last,
being part of the world's future,
  not the painful past."

"Once 'THE FLYING COLORS,'
     now a fading rainbow,
once the biggest canyon,
     now, only an echo."

"I will miss you dear Braniff,
     it's plain to see,
I'll miss you even more,
     my Braniff family."

"So, I bury you dear Braniff,
     family cries in sorrow,
we'll look back on memories,
     but look ahead for tomorrow."

"Questions"

"How do you tell that special someone,
    with everything to give,
this sickness deep within you totals,
    six months to live?"

"How do you tell that special someone
    so dear to your heart,
the love holding us together
    will soon pull apart?"

"How do you plan and prepare,
    how do you adjust,
who can you turn to, and
    who can you trust?"

"When that fight deep within you,
    is overpowered by pain,
sending signals of distress,
    to the master brain."

"So great is that final challenge,
    the challenge or death,
all must face and fight it,
    till the very last breath."

"So please take each single hour, of
    each, and every single day,
live life to its fullest, before
    death takes its prey."

"My New Job"

"Who'd ever, ever guess,
　　who'd ever know,
I'd be a security officer,
　　for Trammell Crow?"

"Midnight at the oasis,
　　I secured my beat,
looking for any movement,
　　trying to be neat."

"Checking every nook and cranny
　　while walking my post,
hoping not to encounter anything,
　　resembling a ghost."

"Knowing I'm all by myself,
　　the elevators talk to me,
each floor a noise of its own,
　　making itself known to me."

"My building and I are wide awake
　　while the city sleeps,
noise-making doors and windows are
　　giving me the creeps."

"Making my routine inspection,
　　walking all the floors,
looking for 'the out of ordinary,'
　　checking all the doors."

"Going down that checklist,
　　I marked the time,
of exactly where I was,
　　and what did I find."

"My nightly shift report nearly done,
  I looked for my relief,
now it's someone else's turn,
  to be, 'duty chief.' "

"The most happiest of persons,
  security officers delight,
getting through a complete shift,
  with an uneventful night."

"A Test of Love"

"I never thought I'd face death,
    without really dying,
never thought I'd feel tears of pain,
    without really crying."

"My heart is so heavy with sorrow,
    for what's yet to come,
I've cried out every single tear,
    till my body's numb."

"I feel so saddened that life has
    been cut so short,
but those dreams and memories were
    lived from the heart."

"If only I could see with my hands,
    they'd cry a silent tear,
for tender love I feel in your touch,
    when you are near."

"A test of the Lord's faith is
    a test of love,
to pass through those Pearly Gates,
    to the Heavens above."

"So weep no more my love,
    you've everything to gain,
the soul will free the body,
    that caused you pain."

"Later, as I look into the clouds,
    it won't take a while,
picking out that cloud formation,
    wearing your smile."

"Roll Call"

"Tomorrow, when the roll is called up yonder,
    you'll be right there,
standing side by side with God our Father,
    without a single care."

"For you did surely surpass,
    every earthly test,
now have earned the reward,
    of Eternal Rest."

"You will always be remembered for
    the things you've done,
putting everything and everyone first,
    as if the chosen one."

"So caring, you put your heart into
    every single deed,
you cared not of yourself, but
    filling every need."

"Your love for the family was
    deep and strong,
the love was always there whether,
    right or wrong."

"By now you're reunited with Dad,
    whose been waiting so long,
but now two loves are one, with
    you in his song."

"You suffered long and hard and
    you earned your wings,
now when I hear the voice of angels,
    it'll be you that sings."

"You have entered through life's
    Eternal Door,
with God your maker to that,
    'Heavenly Shore.' "

"No more pain and suffering,
    flesh turns into dust,
your soul was saved because of,
    God's loving trust."

"I'll always remember you Mom,
    your love so dear,
all those special memories,
    when you were near."

"One day, I'll cross over that,
    'Great Divide,'
we shall be together once again,
    side by side."

"Want"

"I want to love you tenderly,
     with my lips,
I want to love you gently with
     my fingertips."

"I want to love you when two bodies,
     burn with desire,
I want to feel the raging passion,
     setting minds on fire."

"I want to feel the warmth,
     of your tender kiss,
I want to feel the heartbeat
     as bodies remissness."

"I want to completely relax under
     a starlit night,
I want to gaze into the stars and
     the moon so bright."

"But if what I sincerely want
     is only a game,
that someone is 'imagination' and
     having no name."

"Birthday Girl"

"Twenty-five years ago today,
    you entered this world,
a dainty, crying, precious,
    sweet baby girl."

"You had not a single care,
    as a little tot,
you seemed to give more love,
    than the love you got."

"A call from the principal at school
    caused such alarm,
on the playground at recess,
    you broke your arm."

"As a young lady growing up
    learning to compete,
you gave it your very all,
    but learned defeat."

"You learned to feel love,
    from Mom and Dad,
we both loved you so much,
    even when bad."

"You're blessed with Mom's traits,
    some of Dad's too,
but you're still my little girl,
    I truly love you!"

"Today, you're that same sweet baby girl
    turned into womanhood,
In my past memories I look at you,
    I did something good."

"Mixed Up Chemistry"

"You do something to me
     with those sexy eyes,
you do something special to me,
     and I energize."

"You make me feel the excitement,
     of a warm tender kiss,
the softness of your skin, your touch,
     feelings I could not dismiss."

"Two lips molded into one,
     with passion of fire,
turning two starving bodies into
     one burning desire."

"The nearness of you excites me,
     stirs my chemistry,
my heart pounds out of control,
     and so speedily."

"The touch of your fingertips,
     walking hand-in-hand,
just the very closeness of you
     makes life seem so grand."

"I think of you day-by-day,
     hour-by-hour,
when I reach that crucial point,
     another cold shower."

"Only"

"I want only your heart
    beating against mine,
throbbing like ancient war drums,
    up and down my spine."

"I want only your embrace
    holding me tight,
caressing me gently into
    a lover's delight."

"I want only your pretty eyes
    staring willingly,
gazing deep into mine,
    setting emotions free."

"I want only your tender lips
    pressed against mine,
tasting the sparkling passions, of
    a vintage wine."

"I want only one dream as
    I sleep the night
awakening early morning with
    you in my sight."

"I only want all of your love,
    my whole life through,
to fill that empty shell with
    a lifetime of you."

"Lifetime Valentine"

"I want to frame my thoughts,
    of what I want to say,
on this very special occasion
    this very special day."

"Just like a mental picture,
    coming into view,
visions of lifelong happiness,
    a lifetime of you."

"Cupid! Cupid! You've hit me,
    hit me very hard,
my chemistry is boiling over,
    my feelings bombard."

"Valentine, you've changed my life,
    captured my heart,
and I'll always love you for,
    upsetting my apple-cart."

"I want to be your trainer, buddy,
    lover, and friend,
I want to make lasting memories,
    till life reaches its end."

"I'll care for you in sickness, sadness,
    happiness, and laughter,
to care for you in this life, . . .
    and life thereafter."

"You will be totally mine, . . .
    my Valentine, my treasure,
loving you will be my pride,
    my life, my pleasure."

"Ninth Month, Eleventh Day"
(9-1-1)

"A year has passed since
      we exchanged our vows,
absorbing all of the thrills,
      that true love allows."

"We, as a team together,
      working supply and demand,
striving to reach that goal,
      hand clutching hand."

"So many different obstacles,
      down life's daily path,
some made us teary eyed,
      others a hardy laugh."

"We stuck closely together
      through thick and thin,
facing all of those challenges,
      still love would win."

"With all my heart and body,
      and a gleaming eye,
a tender love so special,
      the harder we try."

"Happy anniversary darling,
      9-1-1 saw us through,
with number one behind us,
      strive for number two."

"You are my companion, lover,
      my best friend,
you're my buddy, my trainer,
      you're my Godsend."